DATE DUE

NOV 1 4 2003		

GAYLORD   PRINTED IN U.S.A.

Lisle, Illinois

Northwestern University

STUDIES IN *Phenomenology &*

Existential Philosophy

Elements for an Ethic

Jean Nabert

Preface by

Translated by

Elements for an Ethic

PAUL RICOEUR

WILLIAM J. PETREK

NORTHWESTERN UNIVERSITY PRESS

1969   EVANSTON

Originally published in French under the title
Eléments pour une éthique, copyright © 1943,
2d edition, copyright © 1962
by Aubier, Editions Montaigne.

William J. Petrek is Associate Professor of Philosophy
and Religion and Director of International Study
at DePauw University, Greencastle, Indiana

Contents

[ix]

Translator's Note

As Professor Ricoeur has remarked, Jean Nabert wanted *Elements for an Ethic* to appear without preface, foreword, or introduction of any kind. The experience of fault, failure, and solitude is the best introduction to his reflection on the ethical life. However, Professor Ricoeur judged, and rightly so, that the reader might welcome an attempt to situate *Elements for an Ethic*, first published in 1943, in the tradition of reflective philosophy and, more particularly, in the totality of Nabert's own personal philosophical endeavor. The translator invokes this same reason to justify, at least partially, two brief notes intended to bring up to date Professor Ricoeur's preface, which was written in 1962 for the second edition of *Elements for an Ethic*. These notes concern a posthumous publication and some mention of critical work on the philosophy of Jean Nabert.

I

In 1966, six years after the death of Jean Nabert, *Le Désir de Dieu*, on which the author had been working at the time of his death, was published.[1] The book represents a selection made by Madame Paule Levert from a larger body of notes. Nabert had drafted them in preparation of a book which was intended to develop ideas expressed in the last article published by him before his death, "Le Divin et Dieu."[2] In *Le Désir de Dieu*, notes of varying length are given a logical arrangement which the editor feels corresponds to Nabert's intentions. However, *Le Désir de Dieu* has a not unexpected, or unwelcome, resemblance

1. *Le Désir de Dieu* (Paris: Aubier, 1966).
2. "Le Divin et Dieu," *Les études philosophiques* (July–September, 1959), pp. 321–32.

[xi]

to the intimate journal of a Maine de Biran or the metaphysical diary of a Gabriel Marcel.

In his preface to *Le Désir de Dieu* Paul Ricoeur relates this posthumous work and its intentions to both *Elements for an Ethic* and the *Essay on Evil*.[3] In a reflective philosophy any meditation on, or experience of, the absolute is linked to the effort of consciousness to obtain possession of its being. *Le Désir de Dieu* should then be viewed as a development especially of what is implied in the chapters on primary affirmation and on sources of veneration in *Elements*. This posthumous work should also be seen as an attempt to strengthen our awareness of the absolute in the presence of the nonjustifiable, which is the disturbing theme of the *Essay on Evil*.

Ricoeur suggests that we allow the article, "Le Divin et Dieu," to guide us through *Le Désir de Dieu*. The Nabert article offers three interrelated directions in which reflection on the absolute must proceed. The first direction is a polemical one: one must reject any idea of a substantial being with divine attributes which would be distinct from the act of reflection through which consciousness strives to gain possession of itself. The second direction requires reflection to develop criteria by which it will judge what is divine. The third and final direction aims at discerning "witnesses to the absolute." *Le Désir de Dieu* is divided by its editor into three parts, corresponding to these three directions of reflective thought.

There is a definite movement from the first through the second and into the third of these directions. Ricoeur sees each phase of the movement as incorporated into the succeeding phase: "reflection erases none of its earlier steps: the criteriology of the divine accompanies throughout recourse to witness, just as substitution of a philosophy of the reflective act for a philosophy of the necessary being accompanies throughout a criteriology of the divine."[4]

II

Critical work on the philosophy of Jean Nabert is still limited in size, if solid in quality. In this respect it imitates, to some extent, the limited and careful work of Nabert himself.

3. To preserve continuity with Ricoeur's preface to *Eléments*, I have chosen to refer to his preface to *Le Désir de Dieu*.
4. *Le Désir de Dieu*, p. 14.

The reader, who may want to explore critical appraisals of the philosophy of Nabert, can most profitably consult three publications among others. *Les Etudes philosophiques* devoted its entire issue of July–September, 1962, to articles on Nabert. In that issue, Paul Ricoeur, who has acknowledged the important influence of Nabert on his own philosophy,[5] develops some ideas set forth in his preface to *Elements* in an article entitled "L'Acte et le signe selon Jean Nabert." The same issue contains a bibliography of works of and about Nabert prepared by Ludovic Robberechts.[6] It also includes an article by Nabert, "La Rencontre de l'absolu: le témoignage," published for the first time.

Paul Naulin, in his massive *L'Itinéraire de la conscience*,[7] has given us a most elaborate introduction to the philosophy of Nabert. After a treatment of the notion of "itinerary of consciousness" and of the nature of the reflective method, Naulin conducts the reader with commentary and summary through each of the major works of Nabert. Such help is certainly welcome in the labyrinth of rich thought but often difficult, and sometimes most unusual, style that the reader finds in the philosophy of Jean Nabert.

Finally, the reader might want to consult two articles by a young Belgian philosopher, Robert Franck: "Les Traits fondamentaux de la méthode de Jean Nabert" and "Deux Interprétations de la méthode de Jean Nabert."[8] In the second article the author challenges the interpretations of Nabert's philosophy made by Ricoeur and Naulin. Franck's quarrel with Ricoeur concerns an interpretation of Nabert's philosophical method. Where Ricoeur sees a discontinuity of method between the three major works of Nabert, Franck sees definite continuity. In Naulin's interpretation, the distinction Naulin makes between natural reflection and philosophical reflection is disputed by Franck. This distinction, in Franck's estimation, prompted Ricoeur to

5. Cf., for example, Paul Ricoeur, *History and Truth* (Evanston: Northwestern University Press, 1965), p. 16.

6. This same author has a doctoral dissertation on Jean Nabert: "Les Grandes Lignes de la philosophie de Monsieur Jean Nabert" (Louvain, 1960, mimeographed).

7. Paul Naulin, *L'Itinéraire de la conscience* (Paris: Aubier, 1963).

8. *Revue philosophique de Louvain*, LXIII (February, 1965), 97–115; LXIV (August, 1966), 416–35.

distinguish methods in Nabert. To Naulin the distinction suggests two complementary movements of an identical method. Franck sees no such distinction in Nabert.

In all translations, choices between equally convincing alternatives have to be made. Such choices are especially difficult when no one of the equally convincing alternatives seems to satisfy. While several such instances could be cited in the translation of this book, I do want in particular to call attention to the translation of *affirmation originaire* as "primary affirmation." In so translating the important notion of Nabert—shared by other contemporary French philosophers—I have agreed with Kelbley. Some translators prefer "originary affirmation," but this seems less happy than "primary." A translation like "origin-al affirmation," which clearly appeals to me, is admittedly awkward. However, it does convey the notion of "origin" in an active sense, which is important for understanding the role of primary affirmation in the existential promotion of values in the life of an individual. This emphasis on origin is supported by Paul Ricoeur in his discussion of primary affirmation in his essay "Negativity and Primary Affirmation." [9]

In translating Jean Nabert's *Eléments pour une éthique* I have trod where others feared to. The thought of Nabert is not easily accessible, and his thought is often forbidding in its density and subtlety. Most translations are imperfect, and this translation is numbered among the imperfect ones. However, the often frustrating and disappointing effort of translation has its own special reward. The reward is something like, and yet differs from, the reward of the reader, which is, in this instance, an initiation into the thought of Jean Nabert.

I wish to thank Mr. James Edie, who invited me to make this translation, and DePauw University, from whom I received a research grant to prepare this manuscript for publication. Finally, I wish especially to thank my wife, Sandy. She helped in the typing of the manuscript at each stage. But more importantly, she quietly understood the burden which a translation can become. That understanding greatly lightened the burden.

Greencastle, Indiana   WILLIAM J. PETREK
January, 1969

9. *History and Truth,* pp. 305–28, especially pp. 324–28.

Elements for an Ethic

Preface

Is it necessary to preface this remarkable book? The author wanted it to be without any preparation whatsoever, without foreword or introduction. In fact, from the very first page the reader is confronted with three experiences, with three feelings—fault, failure, and solitude. In a single thrust, reflection can perceive in these experiences "the twofold relationship disclosed by them, viz., a relationship to a nonbeing diffused in them and a relationship to a certitude which is at the same time a compensation for nonbeing and the foundation of its own limitation" (p. 4).[1]

No preliminary justification is offered for beginning this way; whoever agrees to begin this way finds reasons as he moves ahead. Thought is pulled forward by the deep difference which troubles this initial experience. The entire energy of reflection flows from this difference of potential between the aspiration of its desire to be and the experience "of the resistance which this expansion encounters or of the weaknesses of which the self is guilty" (*ibid.*).

The philosopher of reflection does not seek the radical point of departure. He has already begun, but in the mode of *feeling;* everything has already been experienced, but everything remains to be understood, to be "regrasped"—using the happy phrase of Jean Nabert—clearly and rigorously. These initial feelings are evidence that reflection is desire and not intuition of self, enjoyment of one's being. Reflection is justified as reflection by what seems to precede it, to obscure and limit it. It is this

1. [Page references to *Elements for an Ethic* are to the present English edition, not to the French original.—TRANSLATOR.]

same movement which gets hold of itself within its initial confusion and "directs itself to the affirmation toward which the entire moral experience is ordered" (*ibid.*). For reflective philosophy, to begin is not to state a first truth; it is "to reveal the structures" of what precedes reflection, the structures of spontaneous consciousness. To begin is to show that in this consciousness there is an order which can be understood and which can help one understand why this self has not yet attained satisfaction, why reflection is desire.

This initial relationship of reflection to feeling regulates the entire movement of the book. In the first part, entitled "The Givens of Reflection," lucid consciousness illuminates retroactively the basic feelings which set it in motion. In the second part—"Primary Affirmation"—the ascending movement of this reflective recapturing reaches its summit. The *I am* which animates the desire and which the desire to be seeks to equal is revealed as the truth of reflection itself. "However, the curve of this experience only passes through this summit to turn immediately in the direction assigned to it by action, where this action conspires with inclinations, with nature, to promote values in the world" (*ibid.*). In reflective philosophy there is no repose on some mountain of transfiguration. Because reflection is not an intuitive possession of self, the primary affirmation witnesses to itself only through the very movement which, beginning with desire, promotes the existence of the self at all levels of action. It is necessary for the existence of the self "to imitate and verify as much as possible this primary certitude" (p. 57).

The task of the third part—entitled "Existence"—is to extend this movement of expansion toward the world in order to experience the liberation, "both absolute and unreal" (p. 49), which reflection accomplished in its retrospective movement. In order for this liberation to become real, it must prove its efficacy by freeing particular inclinations from the tyranny of their objects. It must also prove it within the discipline of work, in the building of economic, political, and cultural institutions, in the actual interchange of minds. One is not surprised that by bending toward "works" the curve of experience leads us back finally to feeling. The terminal feeling, unlike fault, failure, and solitude, does not express the *distance* of spontaneous consciousness from the certitude which its desire seeks. This feeling expresses the very presence of this certitude, despite the invinci-

ble distance of consciousness from itself. This feeling, nearer the
sublime than beatitude, corresponding to an enjoyment of being
which the reflective method does not offer, is called "veneration"
by Jean Nabert (pp. 191 ff.). It is born of diverse, but secretly
related, examples of greatness: "When absolute actions imply
willingness to lose one's life, they arouse our highest veneration.
. . . This veneration is inspired by the feeling that the being
which we venerate is worthwhile beyond all value through that
which is, in fact beyond all value, and that we go through it
toward what is at the origin of our being. It presents us with
what reflection had us affirm" (pp. 191–92).

Reflection, then, begins with feeling and returns to feeling,
but from a confused feeling to an informed feeling, from a
feeling of separation to one of participation. However, even
though reflection begins with feeling, it remains that free initiative without which life would be neither understood nor
changed. Consequently, although reflection is not everything, it
remains something. Reflection is "a moment within the history
of the desire constitutive of our being" (p. 4).

This is why this book was published without a preface:
reflection finds its preface in feeling. Therefore, there is no need
to place anything whatsoever before what life has already placed
there, before what spontaneous consciousness has already lived.

Now that the death of the master has closed out the cycle of
his work, perhaps it is permissible to write a preface which
would not have the useless pretension of introducing one to the
philosophical themes themselves but which would limit itself to
situating this book in the tradition of reflective philosophy.

Jean Nabert himself gave us the tools to do this job in the
article he wrote on reflective philosophy in 1957 for the *Encyclopédie Française* (19.04–14—19.06–3). In that article he distinguished two orientations. Leaving aside reflection "in which the
absolute reflects itself in the movement of an individual consciousness," he retains only that reflection "which constitutes the
subject itself, first of all, and then recaptures the laws and norms
of spiritual activities in all domains immanent in these operations. . . . What is proper to reflection thus understood is always
to consider the human spirit in its acts and in what it produces
in order to appropriate their meaning. It does this, first of all,
essentially, in the act through which the subject reassures itself
about itself, about its power and its truth." Maine de Biran,

Lachelier, Lagneau, and Brunschvicg belong to this second orientation. In all of them one finds the same coincidence of reflective action with intuition, which grasps its truth. One finds the same power to posit and to renew the act which begins reflection, the same ability to catch hold of the first efforts in which immediate and prereflective consciousness prefigures and suggests reflection.

Within this common method of immanence Jean Nabert sees philosophies of reflection subdividing according to the choice of act to which primary reflection addresses itself.

In a very pedagogical manner, Jean Nabert begins with the Cartesian cogito, which he sees inclining either toward Kant or toward Maine de Biran, depending on whether reflection gives its attention to the operations which constitute true experience in order to discover within them the structures of a transcendental subject, of a universal thought, or whether reflection seeks "to deepen or to liberate the inner life of the self."

Where is Jean Nabert to be located? With Maine de Biran? Yes, if one accepts that all his work, from *The Inner Experience of Freedom* [2] to the *Essay on Evil*,[3] tends to distinguish between *reflection* and *critique*. The principal task of a critique is to disassociate the a priori conditions of the possibility of experience from all empirical genesis and from all a posteriori accretions. In this sense, the moral philosophy of Kant is still a critique in that it constructs the reflective analysis of good will according to the model used by the reflective analysis of true knowledge. It is this parallelism which requires one to separate, in one's search for the principle of morality, the a priori from the empirical and, by way of consequence, the formalism of duty from the pathology of desire. Formalism in moral philosophy is then the result of the transposition onto the practical level of a critique of knowledge. It simply brings into the domain of action the distinction between the transcendental and the empirical which belongs to the critique. By developing a *reflection on action*, conceived as irreducible to any critique of knowledge, Jean Nabert undeniably takes up a position in the tradition of Maine de Biran. Even more, by applying reflection to the move-

2. [*L'Expérience intérieure de la liberté* (Paris: Presses Universitaires de France, 1924).—TRANSLATOR.]

3. [*Essai sur le mal* (Paris: Presses Universitaires de France, 1955).—TRANSLATOR.]

ment by which we attempt to appropriate for ourselves the primary affirmation from which we are in some manner separated or from which we have fallen, Jean Nabert rediscovers a meaning of "Ethics" which is closer to Spinoza than it is to Kant. To the distinction between critique and reflection corresponds a similar distinction between moral philosophy and ethic. Since Kant, moral philosophy uses the idea of duty; this idea is inseparable from a "critique" of good will which disassociates the rational form of the imperative from the matter of desire. In this sense, the ethic of Jean Nabert is not at all a moral philosophy. Ethic means for him the reasoned history of our effort to exist, of our desire to be. The curve of reflection, which in *Elements for an Ethic* moves between fault and veneration and passes through primary affirmation, is in no way borrowed from a "critique" of knowledge. It expresses the irreducibility of the personal self to a transcendental subject. Jean Nabert also vehemently challenges this idea of Lachelier: "As far as I am concerned, I cannot conceive of a thinking subject except as a reflection of objective thought or of truth on itself" (*Lettres*, p. 81).[4]

However, Jean Nabert cannot be included among the descendants of Maine de Biran. Maine de Biran "failed to bring out of the experience of the primitive fact the forms and the categories of objective knowledge and to guarantee their value." In opposition to Maine de Biran, then, one must maintain the plurality of "areas of reflection." One must abandon all reciprocal genesis of norms regulating knowledge and science and operations by which the self appropriates for itself its spiritual causality. The consequence is important: it is because reflection on action cannot give birth to a critique of knowledge that the two modes of reflection can aid each other. "A just conception of the relationships between reason and consciousness depends on their solidarity." This "complementarity of reflective analysis applied to the order of knowledge and of reflective analysis applied to the domain of action" distinguishes Nabert both from the critique which reduces the "dimension of inwardness" to transcendental knowledge and from Biranism, which professes

4. [*Oeuvres de Jules Lachelier* (Paris: Alcan, 1933).—TRANSLATOR.]

to derive transcendental consciousness with its exigencies of objectivity from the primitive fact of willing.

Because of this "solidarity" between consciousness and reason, reflection is not trapped in the irrational. Feeling itself has its "structures," in which the itinerary of freedom can unfold an exemplary history, which can be "understood." The necessity of this reasoned history, which follows from its relationship to primary affirmation, assures the continual coincidence of the existential with the rational. The declarations of the article in the *Encyclopédie* echo *Elements for an Ethic:* "For every individual his history is the history of this desire, of the radical ignorance of self in which he is at first, of the errors into which he allowed himself to be dragged, of the seductions which abused him, and, throughout the failures which he undergoes, of the light finally thrown on his true orientation. No matter how contingent this history is for every consciousness, an ethic must determine its essential moments and thus aid in the illumination of the deep will of the individual. . . . An ethic can only offer itself as the structure of a concrete history which each self begins again and which it does not always complete" (*Elements*, p. 117). This is why the heritage of Maine de Biran cannot be exploited unless the reflective method, freed from the domination of the critique, still remains in the intellectual aura of critical philosophy. The *Encyclopédie* article says it well: "It was necessary for a critical theory of knowledge to establish the priority in the 'I think' of its function of objectivity and truth so as to keep reflection, immediately attentive to the concrete forms of inner experience, from indulging in sterile irrationalism."

It is tantalizing to compare the *via media* of Jean Nabert—between Kant and Maine de Biran—to Husserlian phenomenology. Certain aspects of the reflective method invite one to do so. In particular, a prescription of the *Encyclopédie* article resounds like a Husserlian theme: "The task . . . is to reveal the intimate relationship between the act and the significations in which it objectifies itself. . . . The reflective analysis demonstrates its fecundity by getting hold of the moment in which the spiritual act incarnates itself in a sign which immediately risks turning against it." *The Inner Experience of Freedom* already applied this prescription to a theory of motivation (pp. 123–55), a theory which has lost none of its strength. In this theory we see the discontinuous initiatives of spiritual causality produced in the continuity of a series of motivations which unfold consciousness at the level of facts: "The causality of consciousness, unrepresentable in itself, and always in advance of its expression, must incarnate itself through motives in the tissue of psychological life in order to reveal its content to us" (p. 132). This objectification does not represent a disgrace for freedom or a comedy of bad faith. On the contrary, this objectification makes of our motives *signs,* in which we can learn what we have willed, through which we can speak, communicate, and justify to others the meaning of our acts. Certainly, by designating the initiatives of our self by what we have called the meaning of the willed, which is nothing else but the meaning of our motives, we present it for an objective, scientific, and determinist reading. Nabert used the term "law of representation" to designate this exigency in accordance with which our free causality expresses itself and reveals its content through a series of motivations which have to appear as a determinist chain: "If motives are, as we have said, the expression of an act, if they unfold the act in representation, they cannot be detached completely from the act from which they issue, no matter how inclined we are to make them depend on psychological antecedents. Through them the action of consciousness develops. Through them we know what we have willed, or rather we can know if we seek in them the signs of an actual willing instead of considering them as givens which do not involve the causality of the subject" (p. 129). This theory of motivation was the first actualization of that rule of the reflective method which, according to the article in the *Encyclopédie,* consists in "getting hold of the moment in which the spiritual act incarnates itself in a sign which immediately risks turning against it."

The very original theory of values in Chapter 5 of *Elements for an Ethic* is related to the same conception of the rapport between act and sign. The apparent objectivity of values is due to the necessity for freedom to pass through the mediation of history and of works. The self is required to appropriate indirectly what reflection grasps and affirms as pure consciousness of self. The self appropriates this as the value of a work. In this Nabert sees both a "promotion" and an "obfuscation": a promotion of values themselves and an obfuscation of the generative principle of value (p. 58). "Value is always linked to a certain obfuscation of the principle on which it is based and which sustains it. Value would not be value if it did not have in it something which makes us think that it does not exhaust the principle which it symbolizes or verifies. . . . Promotion of value can only be indirect. In this respect, the obfuscation of the generative principle of value is the expression of a law which affects all manifestations of the human spirit. What Maine de Biran says about signs, that is, about acts which reveal its constitutive power to consciousness, must also be said about values . . .; every creative act can promote value, and esteem and know itself, only if it agrees to involve itself in an effort, in an action, where at first we lose track of it" (*ibid.*).

The importance of this theory of signs in Nabert should not be underestimated. What he often calls "verifying" the primary affirmation is also "symbolizing" it.

This positive comparison of the reflective method and phenomenology, suggested by this theory of signs, is, however, provisional. The opposition between them, which finally wins out, is really very revelatory of the final intention of the reflective method according to Nabert. The meditating subject in the phenomenological analysis seems to Nabert to behave like a pure "regard" directed to values, essences, and objective significations (*Encyclopédie* article). However, in order for the phenomenological analysis to offer these significations of consciousness as a kind of spectacle, it was necessary "that the bond between the act and the signification which seemed to be one with the work had to be loosened." Phenomenology would then miss "the real life of acts grasped in their birth and in their first attempts." It follows that phenomenology will by preference be attentive "to the signification already detached from the primary act." Whatever one might think of this objection, which strictly speaking has weight only with regard to the most static descriptions of phenomenology, it is above all revelatory of the true intentions of the reflective method. Because the ambition of the reflective method is to get hold once again of pure acts, through signs in which they reveal their signification, it never aims at a simple description but at a reappropriation of the primary affirmation by a consciousness which discovers itself dispossessed of that affirmation. Its theory of signs or symbols immediately has an ethical significance. The problem of expression is from the very beginning one of "obfuscation" of the human spirit by the signs which are necessary for the "verification" of the primary affirmation in human experience, in a history, and in works. Reflective philosophy can say that "it appropriates symbolic thought and the multiple relationships between significative intentions and signifying modes." It seeks to have understanding of self, based on "the text which its actions have constituted" (*Elements for an Ethic*, p. 3), coincide with "a regeneration of its being" (*ibid.*).

This ethical accent of the reflective method is most pronounced in the present volume. It does not give forth its fullest flavor in *The Inner Experience of Freedom*. In the *Essay on Evil* it is submerged by another accent, which, for want of a better term, I shall call hyperethical. In this respect, *Elements for an Ethic* represents not only the middle work of the master but the canonical work of the reflective method.

If *The Inner Experience of Freedom* remains inferior to the reflective level attained in *Elements for an Ethic*, it is not only because that work gives an important place to discussions and refutations, which are entirely absent from *Elements for an Ethic*, and breaks a difficult trail between the illusions of free will, understood as psychological contingency, and determinism. It is not because that book remains corrective and argumentative but because it is still torn between two points of view which tend toward a more intimate union in *Elements for an Ethic*. The idea of freedom is first of all attained by reflection before the experience in which it is verified is constituted. This is why "categories of freedom" (pp. 188 ff.) [5]—fatality of character, order of personality, infinity of sacrifice—belong to a second reflection, more concrete than the first. They express the structure of "a belief which narrates the history of our freedom" (p. 188). "By becoming the history of a belief, the inner experience of freedom also becomes the history of the ideas through which this belief, in escaping the pure subjectivity of feeling, manifests the categories of freedom. Each of these ideas or categories works like a crystallization of the belief" (p. 189). Therefore, a duality remains between the philosophical concept and the experience of freedom. This duality is even championed by the method proper to the thesis of 1924: "We do not, however, wish to say that freedom is substantially identical to the belief which we form

5. [Page references in this paragraph are to *The Inner Experience of Freedom*, French edition.—TRANSLATOR.]

concerning it. Freedom is nothing if it is not characteristic of psychological causality" (pp. 193–94). Thus freedom cannot be given in an experience; "freedom can be found only in the idea of an act whose psychological elements we have produced" (p. 194). But, on the other hand, if this idea is not to remain "an entirely speculative hypothesis," it must have recourse to the "mediating function" of belief. Thus belief, "by bringing together our reflection on this act and the history of our freedom" (p. 194) hides the hiatus between reflection and experience. It succeeds quite well in doing so because of the structure of this belief, because of the "categories" which guarantee the passage from reflection to experience. But the hiatus is only hidden: in its source the history of freedom is distinct from reflection.

Elements for an Ethic wants to erase this difference. Beginning with fault, failure, and solitude, reflection nourishes itself directly on these feelings, which correspond to the history of freedom in the preceding work. No direct reflection on psychological causality gives us an idea of freedom prior to spontaneous consciousness. Perhaps this is also why the vocabulary changes from one book to the other: it is no longer the history of freedom but the history of this desire to be, "whose deepening is identified with ethic itself" (p. 117). "An ethic can only offer itself as the structure of a concrete history which each self begins again and which it does not always complete" (*ibid.*).

Elements for an Ethic, then, tends toward this unity of method to which the article in the *Encyclopédie* gives us the key. Does *Elements* succeed? One might question whether all duplication has ceased between the highest certitude, which Nabert himself says is "both absolute and unreal" (p. 49), and action: "The absolute affirmation which affirms itself within my affirmation then produces both a certitude and an appeal. The appeal is addressed to the self in order that, in the world and within duration, through duty and, if necessary through sacrifice, it verify the I am and make a reality of it. This certitude is the actuality of a relationship which neither failures nor forgetfulness affect because it is immanence within I am of an affirmation which surpasses all multiplicity as well as erases all separation between subjects" (*ibid.*). Are not certitude and appeal a duplication, just as earlier the idea of freedom and the history of freedom were?

Even supposing this equilibrium of the reflective method to

have existed, it had to be broken. This time it was not due to a handling of the reflective method but to an experience, to a feeling—the feeling of the nonjustifiable—which can no longer be treated as a "given of reflection" (as understood in the first part of *Elements for an Ethic*). The nonjustifiable is that unaccountable face of evil which can no longer be reflectively recognized as resistance or weakness and which is, consequently, no longer homogeneous and proportionate to our desire to be. It no longer represents a symmetry which I might understand by opposing it to the experience of valid norms. These are evils rooted in a contradiction more radical than that between valid and invalid. Consequently, to speak of the nonjustifiable, the reflective method can no longer be satisfied to penetrate with reason the feeling of dissatisfaction which is nourished by consciousness of fault, failure, and solitude. A new tactic is needed to suggest something beyond the nonvalid. It will be suggested through the nonvalid, by a method of transparency and going the limit: "These are evils, these are disruptions of the inner being, conflicts and sufferings without conceivable solace." Thus, just as the nonjustifiable exceeds, from below, the nonvalid, according to normative thought, so the desire for justification exceeds from on high all effort of moral rectitude, as this same normative thought prescribes it. The nonjustifiable requires a reconciliation which transcends all norms.

However, it would be a mistake to oppose the *Essay on Evil* to *Elements for an Ethic*. The *Essay* explodes a moral rationalism which would refer all actions, all feelings, and all judgments to norms. But this moral rationalism does not in any way characterize the *Elements*. In it duty is "deduced" very late in the book (Chapter 8) as an "aid" for the desire to be. It belongs to the essential history of this desire: "The moral imperatives, the order of duty in general, are a moment in this history, whose significance it is incumbent upon an ethic to deduce and determine" (p. 117). The *Essay on Evil* accomplishes its effort of rupture only by relying on a derivative moment of the ethic, the moment of law, of rule, of norm, which in the *Elements* was established only "to block the centrifugal forces which aggravate the inner dissension of tendencies and the opposition of individuals" (p. 120).

If the desire for justification of the *Essay on Evil* goes further than the effort of regeneration of the *Elements,* this is because it comes to life in an experience of norms which is not the fundamental experience of an ethic. There is no question here of wanting to deny the newness of tone, both tragic and more religious, of the *Essay on Evil*. But it would be entirely erroneous to see in the *Essay* a refutation of *Elements* or even simply a new phase of the reflective method which breaks with the preceding phase. On the contrary, evocation of the nonjustifiable and recourse to the desire for justification allow one to explore the confines and the limits of this reflection, one principal "area" of which was recognized by *Elements for an Ethic*.

PAUL RICOEUR

BOOK I
The Givens of Reflection

1 / The Experience of Fault

THERE ARE TWO WAYS to treat historical events. One way aims at a determinist explanation, the other seeks to recapture the decisions, moral energy, and ideals expressed by the events. The self does something similar in treating its own past. It can strive for knowledge of its own history while freeing itself from all self-interest. However, it can seek, not only to recapture and understand itself by reading the text which its actions have constituted, but also to make this understanding coincide with a regeneration of its being. Through reflection, better than it could in action, the self hopes to discern in the cooperating and opposing forces which constitute its past what belongs to nature and what belongs to an aspiration which transcends nature. The act of reflection is already evidence that the self grasps and affirms itself as a power, creative of history, binding a pure self which makes up the entire moral substance of its being and a nature which it can neither disavow nor repudiate without condemning itself to impotency and unreality.

Even though reflection is the result of free initiative, it remains linked to feelings which accompany the total moral experience and have initially for consciousness an enigmatic character. Everything happens as if the self could neither flourish outside action and communication of minds nor keep action and communication from recreating and intensifying the desire from which they issue. Also, everything happens as if action and communication could only give rise to disappointment, whose strangeness astonishes the self, or occasion a feeling of fault, to which consciousness risks succumbing unless it sees within it an

[3]

opportunity for self-understanding. These feelings nourish reflection, they are its matter; they make reflection, although free, appear as a moment within the history of the desire that is constitutive of our being.

Most of the feelings engendered by the expansion of the self are linked to the fundamental experiences of solitude, failure, and fault. They are signs of the resistance which this expansion encounters or of the weaknesses of which the self is guilty. These weaknesses and this resistance also give us insight into the aspiration which actuates desire and into the certitude which sustains it and toward which it tends. Immanent in moral experience, reflection on failure, fault, and solitude not only reveals the structures permitting us to understand the limits of satisfaction; it also directs itself to the affirmation toward which the entire moral experience is ordered. However, the curve of this experience only passes through this summit to turn immediately in the direction assigned to it by action, where this affirmation conspires with inclinations, with nature, to promote values in the world. Experiencing its own contingency, consciousness, by reflecting on its past, can propose to discover beneath this contingency, beneath the accidents and particularities which have affected its own life, the elements of fault, failure, and solitude and the twofold relationship disclosed by the experience of them, viz., a relationship to a nonbeing diffused in them and a relationship to a certitude which is at the same time a compensation for nonbeing and the foundation of its own limitation.

One of the most mysterious phenomena of moral life is the surprise that consciousness experiences after action, not only in no longer being for itself what it was before action but in no longer being able to disassociate the idea of its own causality from the memory of the particular act which it accomplished. An isolated action has affected the causality of the entire self and has robbed it of the possibility of recovering its integrity. One might attempt to account for this astonishment by the narrow range of attention at the moment of the act. It is true that, as long as it is turned toward the representation of the act, consciousness is blocked from grasping causality, which is exercised in the generation of an idea as well as in decision. One might also reflect on the solidarity of acts and on the solidarity of consciousness with all of them. However, this way one will not understand how impotent the self now finds itself to break

down its causality, just as its particular actions seemed frag-
mented or separated. This causality revealed its quality in a
single action. Memory recreates unceasingly a simultaneity of
the interior act by which consciousness judges itself and of the
past act which is the matter for this memory. The act of remembering, which it seemed should liberate it, makes consciousness
a prisoner of itself. Instead of a causality which could offer its
service after each action, there appears a causality which has
affected itself, which does not know how to deliver itself from
itself.

A transfer is produced from the quality of a particular action
to the causality of the self. The negative predicate of value
attributed to the action transfers to the causality of the acting
subject, communicates itself to the entire self. Henceforth, consciousness seems hemmed in by these alternatives: either no
longer to separate the causality of the self from the quality of the
accomplished action or to disavow oneself and by forgetfulness
attempt a kind of break with one's being. When man turns
toward the memory of his experiences, he discovers there are
very few which do not give the lie to any pretension he might
have had of being equal to himself. Will he allow himself to be
seduced by the hope of a radical change? Will he sink deeper
into despair or into a sort of indifference regarding his own
being? For consciousness to accept this would be to accept self-
defeat. Consciousness can save itself only by using the memories
of its experiences and the interior opposition they have introduced into consciousness as matter for reflection, giving it a hold
on its own causality not permitted by action in the course of
accomplishment. Rather than allow its memories to waste away,
the self will rely on them to deepen the feeling, at first confused,
of a constantly renewed experience of difference between the
real unfolding of its being in the world and the idea of a causality where it would truly be equal to itself.

In the beginning the feeling of fault is linked to well-defined
actions implying the transgression of a rule, of a duty, and
including ascertainable consequences. The determination of actions which have not been such as duty required, their discontinuity, the more or less clear hierarchy of their seriousness, all
contrive to suggest that the feeling of fault is contained in the
relationship between a decision of the subject and a rule. These
factors also contrive to suggest that, correlative to fault which

one might call objective, this feeling of fault expresses the way in which consciousness suffers interiorly the choice it has made. Still, there is a singular contrast between the finite character of the obligation or action and the kind of global condemnation of our being which accompanies or is fused with the feeling of fault. No matter how episodic our action has been, no matter how loosely linked it has been to the permanent and lasting options of the self, through the suffering which it occasions action provokes a fundamental questioning of our value. Our effort fails to contain the feeling of fault within the limits of the action which provoked it. One might say that what is proper to moral life, as opposed to other forms of activity, is not to limit the influence on consciousness of each of our actions.

This is what is misunderstood by an interpretation of the feeling of fault which pretends to see in it only the affective and transient trace of a judgment made of our action which we recognize at the same time as ours and as contrary to a law. In this judgment consciousness would acknowledge its responsibility and would even offer itself for punishment. But it would do so in such a way that, immediately recovering mastery of self, it would not have to consider, behind the quality of its action, the quality of the causality from which its action issued. The feeling of fault would not go beyond this relationship between an action indicted by judgment and a causality which its own actions would always leave available. It would be as though, in exercising itself, this causality did not affect itself in its foundations. However, with this hypothesis, one has trouble explaining how it is that the feeling of fault disengages itself so easily from action, in its intrinsic and objective immorality, to become concentrated in an absolute appraisal which the self makes of itself. Is there nothing more in all this than a kind of diffusion of fault over the self, provoking the feeling of a diminution of our being and a loss of our moral integrity? Is there nothing to search for beyond this diffuse participation of the whole person in an act and in a fault which have altered the relationship of moral values? Just as a certain disgust arises from certain contacts, so there would be a disgust with self arising out of even minor faults. This disgust would arise, not so much because the self would have returned to the source of its acts, but because the quality which these acts owe to moral values would transmit itself by a sort of contagion to the being of the whole self. Besides, this contamination would be favored by the very powerful tendency to seek out an author for accomplished actions. The quality of these actions would involve the subject, who would feel himself affected by it.

Even though this interpretation does contain some truth, it cannot exhaust the experience of fault; rather, it remains at the threshold of the problem. Indeed, the experience of fault would not coincide in so many respects with the history of consciousness of self if, while relative to moral values, it did not have deeper roots and if it did not actually involve an experience of another order which moral life only specifies and determines. Even though the feeling of fault is produced at the time of a single action, in relation to a definite rule or obligation, it goes beyond the feeling of responsibility or transgression which is imputable to us. This feeling of fault is supported and sustained by a feeling which mixes with it and melts into it so well that we have some difficulty in isolating it, even though it expresses the relationship of the self to what is at the origin of all consciousness of self.

From this point of view, what reflection of the self on fault and on its past must allow us to discover is the real order of the conditions of feelings and experiences which we include under the single title of moral experience. The preponderance acquired by certain givens involved in social life and in the relations of minds in the total sphere of their reciprocal duties contrives to mask the energy of more fundamental feelings, without which the first would not succeed in touching the human soul so profoundly. When the feeling of fault breaks away from the forms which it assumes when linked to interdictions and forbidden things which have nothing especially moral about them, it seems, in fact, to involve itself in a self-sufficient experience. More generally, it is a remarkable fact that the unfolding of each of the functions of the human spirit in a direction which confirms or reinforces the autonomy of each function and draws it away from solidarities earlier enjoyed with other functions tends also to break its ties with a more essential experience, which involves the highest interests of existence. There is a certain rationalization of moral experience which rapidly impoverishes it. This rationalization, which is careful to purge moral experience of everything only accidentally or primitively joined to it, neglects going back to more hidden sources of moral experience. Primitive and impure forms of moral experience tend to hide something in themselves which was already profound but which can reveal itself fully only as their function matures.

This is sufficient to suggest the tenacity with which representations, which enlarge its significance, and feelings, which link it to religious experience, adhere to the consciousness of fault despite the rationalization or the autonomy of moral experience. A great difficulty for reflection arises out of this. While one risks mutilating the experience of fault by a rationalization too narrow for it, there is no less a danger and temptation to make it completely solidary with a well-determined form of the religious life—and, in this fashion, to some degree contingent on it—and solidary, too, with both the doctrine which sustains the religious life and the feelings which accompany it. It is indeed impossible to get around this difficulty. Such an impossibility proves, better than anything else, how much the feeling of fault goes beyond a moral experience strictly limited to itself. But it is a fact that fundamental feelings of the human soul, realizing close ties with different doctrinal interpretations and with different currents of civilization, take on such varied forms and in appearance become so much unlike themselves that it seems a vain enterprise to seek to determine a permanent and universal structure for them. Where can we find characteristics common to the agony of a consciousness tortured by the memory of sin, dissatisfied with all expiation, and to the lucid avowal of a weakness which a corrected judgment will repair, or to a tranquil acceptance of its being by a consciousness which experiences no displeasure "in being neither angel nor Cato"? Besides, if the experience of fault in its innermost reality participates in the nature of religious and metaphysical experience which gives fault its truth and its foundation, then perhaps the experience of fault began to inform religious and metaphysical experience before being informed by them. The determinative action of the experience of fault is not inferior to its plasticity. One can discover it at the origin of certain religious movements and of certain individual conversions. Sometimes a contrast breaks out between the intimate givens of consciousness and the feelings which it ought to experience in order to be in accord with faith or with the doctrine it professes. It is then necessary to get hold of the experience of fault before it is seized upon by a doctrine or by a faith which bends it in a particular direction. This doctrine or faith would have us accept as immediate givens feelings which often they will have enriched but which sometimes they will in part have constituted. When reflection believes it has grasped these feelings in their greatest purity, it discovers that all the elements of consciousness of self are found in them in such a way that, unable to remain within themselves, these feelings always surround acts contemporaneous with the formation of a religion or a philosophy. The deepening of these feelings prevents them from remaining in isolation from one another and helps to discern the inner acts with which they are solidary.

It seems, then, that within the experience of fault the relationship of consciousness to its past cannot be separated from the movement of reflection which must both disclose the conditions of consciousness of self and return the self to possession of its being. Far from being a sterile return to a distant past, reflection is not distinguished from the operations by which the self gets hold of itself at the very moment that it attempts to go to the roots of its being. The moments of reflection are for the self the moments of its liberation because they advance it toward the certitude which is the source of all its hope.

What consciousness experiences from the very start is the impossibility in which it finds itself of appropriating wholly the productive causality of the action which it considers a fault. Behind intentions and motives which allow examination, it only touches in some way upon a causality which it can neither disavow, as though it were not its own, nor make entirely clear to itself. It sees well enough the evil which is in its action; it does not succeed in getting hold of the evil which is in its causality and without which the evil which is in its action would not have been produced. It reassures itself that neither its intentions nor its motives, which afford matter for its judgment, would have been efficacious without consent, without a more interior act. But this act, which nevertheless has divided the self against itself, eludes us. To say that causality should not have chosen this act is only to express in another way the feeling of fault. To transfer to causality the quality of the action which indicts consciousness is to introduce a hidden quality in which one can see an indication of perversion of the will, in the presence of which all reflection must stop and acknowledge its impotency.

All the same, the fact that the experience of fault is profiled against the background of a larger and more constant experience can aid reflection in its beginnings. There is no definitive act to which fault relates, and there is not much sense in talking about diffused fault. However, after we have satisfied what duty required of us, nothing is more real than the feeling that we have remained inadequate to ourselves and that we have not responded to a secret appeal which we hear. We know that we refuse to accede to obligations which neither our status nor our set of duties defines and which might perhaps become for us the occasion for development of the constitutive desire of our being. Is this not simply a mirage? Would we still experience a dissatisfaction of the same order at the level of freely sought and freely accepted obligations? It could be. But this dissatisfaction only becomes the richer with meaning. It translates the disappointment of a consciousness in which the feeling of fault is first of all related to the memory of actions contrary to duty and also to possibilities of action which were passed up. But, beyond both of these, it relates to the experience of an ever renewed difference between what really makes up the causality of the self and what it should be capable of in order for the self to be equal to its true being. It is an indication of the same order that we perceive in the desire to atone for the fault by particular acts and reparations having no common measure with the size and importance of the fault itself, as though we were offered no other way for discovering the integrity of our being.

Reflection, which as it unfolds verifies the impossibility of disassociating the operation by which we save ourselves and the operation by which we discover the principle which saves us, proceeds, indeed, from an exigency of integrity. No other reflection can similarly guarantee its own progress and the affirmation which terminates it. From the very beginning, the verification which it makes of its own advance coincides with the beginning of an inner regeneration of consciousness and of a mustering of its forces. Between the enunciation and the principle, between the operation which discerns it and the act by which consciousness takes possession of itself, the gap is closed to such a degree that it leaves no room for doubt or hesitation. By thus endowing with a universal character both the principle which it attains and the very experience which leads toward it, reflection does not exceed its own powers. The most general conditions of human experience can only be immanent in reflection which both discovers them and, in discovering them, engenders a new birth of consciousness.

The desire for regeneration is not a disavowal or a forgetting of the past; on the contrary, it includes a relationship, unceasingly maintained, of the self to its past. But what kind of consciousness is capable of both condemning its past and itself and experiencing in the depths of itself an invincible aspiration which makes it refuse to think that all hope of restoration of its being is henceforth forbidden to it? As long as the self is for itself identically the self which defines its past and the self which seeks to appropriate this past so as not to succumb to the feeling of fault, it can only find itself faced with itself and its past, without recourse against either. Its very effort makes it contemporary with this past which destroyed its integrity. However, a relation of the self to God, who dwells in it, breaks into the distress of a self which understands itself only as identified with a past which it condemns. This relation either compensates for the relation to one's past or overcomes it. The being of the self is defined, is constituted, by these two relationships, viz., by a relationship to a past where always, to some degree, its liberty is involved and by a relationship to the principle from which it draws its desire for existence and its strength for regeneration. Reflection, which in the beginning is identified with the judgment which the self makes of itself, can only continue with the deepening of this double relationship. But, through the second of these relationships, it seems that reflection can liberate if the judgment it makes of itself is identically the judgment which an absolute consciousness would make. In its feeling of fault the self can be optimistic only if subsequent reflection manifests an unconditional certitude from which the self could draw the power not so much to absolve itself as to draw a little closer to its own being.

On the other hand, it is only through fault, and by reflection on fault, that the self discovers not only its own past but, behind it, a past which goes beyond the limits of its memories and of all its empirical history. Without wanting in any way to attenuate the importance of any of its initiative, consciousness discerns that this initiative was not sufficient to produce fault. It could do so only if it encountered the secret complicity of a much more remote past which opposes an absolute limit to any ambition one might have of understanding it or of recapturing its genesis. One might say that this past only enters consciousness or becomes accessible to it thanks to fault. It is liberty within fault which discerns and confirms the presence of this remote past and makes it such that the relationship of consciousness to its past is never a relationship to a nature which would be object, determinism, nonself for a subject. What idealism in all its forms tends to assimilate, reduce, or resolve into inadequate knowledge is what the experience of fault discovers as irreducible and refractory to all deduction and all rationalization. It discovers the participation of the self in a past whose weight it increases by its own faults but which insinuates itself into all actions of the self and delays or obstructs the development of its own aspiration. The fault individualizes this past without creating it. There is no origin which can be empirically assigned to it. But this past can be compared to the past to which reflection on fault gives meaning. For, just like it, this past enjoys authenticity only by its possible relationship to a self which finds this past in the depths of all its efforts.

Certainly, it is below any assignable fault that the self reflectively touches upon a past mixed with its own. However, even though one cannot qualify this past in any way which would introduce it into the realm of value judgments, it keeps consciousness from affirming that it has touched the depths of a resistance in which its responsibility is in no way involved. Discovered in relation to the feeling of fault, it is not a nonbeing indifferent to the destiny of the self. If it is particularized only in our own past and acts, this helps us to understand why our feeling of fault stands out, as we said, against a background of a larger experience which surrounds moral experience. We take charge of the nonbeing that is in us because we find it impossible to detect the point where the help we freely give it ceases. We do not allow ourselves to think that, without our participation, this nonbeing arouses our feeling of fault or that we have radically abolished its presence in our decisions.

Therefore, it is true that moral experience is not limited to personal faults which we remember but is tied to a fundamental metaphysical experience. However, it communicates to this metaphysical experience a tonality which maintains its meaning at the level of the history of consciousness, in the twofold relationship of consciousness to pure action whose idea it must formulate and to a nonbeing which it must conceive as a past always contemporaneous with the destiny it assumes. The life of the self, then, is defined as an oscillation between two limits whose fundamentally practical importance tends to be hidden by a theoretical definition using the notion of absolute contradiction. What is in the self as a nonself is such for the self only in its relationship to a consciousness which would be absolute transparency for itself. Its moral experience becomes for consciousness the source of absolute affirmations which it does not have to borrow from another order.

One might even say, in this respect, that all the ideas by which theoretical thought designates what occasions new resistance to total rationalization derive from an experience that is more metaphysical than moral. The opaqueness of being to knowledge symbolizes, from the point of view of thought, an opaqueness earlier experienced by consciousness in its relationship to the unfolding of a desire for existence. The way in which theoretical thought interprets this fundamental and metaphysically primary experience should not lead us into error as to the real order of their conditioning and their dependence. When, according to its own methods, thought undertakes to reduce the nonbeing it comes up against, it easily forgets that a certain feeling of the inequality of our being with itself is first and that it furnishes the givens from which thought creates its autonomy. There persists, within the categories in which understanding would like to grasp it, the experience of a destiny united to a past which reflection has the right to affirm and recognize without being able to illuminate it completely.

Probing into the depths of this experience transforms the consciousness of fault. This consciousness of fault, even though relative to actions which empirical memories touch on, is tied to a past which, although not the past of the self, has this self participating in a structure of being which cannot be reduced to the operations of individual consciousness. Even though fault does not cease to be imputable to an act of the self, it can no longer be understood solely and exhaustively within the context of this act. This act does not create, all by itself, all the nonbeing which is in fault; the act determines the nonbeing and makes it its own. The nonbeing of fault communicates with an essential nonbeing which transcends the actions of the individual self without attenuating the gravity of the actions for consciousness.

But it follows from this that the self is not imprisoned in meditation on an act which would block its horizon. If, through complacency and weakness, the self has in some way activated the nonbeing in which it participates, it is not for this reason excluded from relationship to an opposite principle which is no less constitutive of its being. Through this twofold relationship which the experience of fault and reflection on fault allows it to sense, consciousness can no longer separate its own being from the incessant movement in which it tends toward misery or purity without ever getting to the depths of misery or the summit of purity. Its faults no longer qualify it with an absolute predicate which would define its being and exclude all hope of regeneration. The choices of consciousness do not lose their weight. However, they give reflection an opportunity to discern in the act a causality which has agreed to be an accomplice of what in the self never ceases to be in opposition to perfect transparence of consciousness. Hope is mixed with a sharper self-awareness of what in the past of the self witnesses, beyond its own act, to a relationship with a more obscure depth. New difficulties and new resistance issue without respite from this depth. The self increasingly desires to overthrow the import of the actions which occasioned reflection. Its present now opens on possibilities for action from which it does not anticipate cancellation of its past but conversion of that past into liberty. However, the interior act by which the self refuses to be defeated by its past and by its faults costs it infinitely more than it would cost it to maintain a self-condemnation which would remain somehow within itself, rejecting any idea of integrity to be reconquered or refashioned. Henceforth, it is necessary for the self to verify at every instant, in its feelings and acts, a conversion to its true being and, at the same time, to doubt its own authenticity and profundity. Its past causes the evidence the self offers to itself to remain, in its own estimation, ambiguous and uncertain.

What is decisive, however, is the transformation which reflection effects in the relationship of consciousness to its past. It is a movement of reflection which is also a promise of liberation. When this reflection begins, the past, one might say, blocks the present. The passage of time seems to have no other role than to bring back the same past and the same memories in such a way that consciousness seems to be unceasingly pulled backwards. Or rather, it moves toward new presents only to become even more subject to the hold of its past. Once reflection succeeds in opposing some resistance to this past, and in restoring to consciousness a joy in and a disposition of its present which is sufficient for the possibility of a future to declare itself, it is the future which progressively conquers the past. It does so not with the intent of abolishing it but of building on it the creation of a law for the proximate history of consciousness. Fault cannot be the starting point of a regeneration of consciousness through the discovery of its principle without permitting or without favoring the discovery of an inner necessity. This inner necessity is capable of enlisting the past in the service of the future of the self in terms of its highest hopes. However, the memory of fault continues for a long time to assail consciousness. It is impossible for it not to make its resistance felt by a self which believes that it has really and totally accomplished its liberation. Self-pardon would contradict the principle which is at the source of its renascent hope and which directs the entire movement of reflection from its most halting beginning.

2 / The Meaning of Failure

FIRST OF ALL, it is necessary to limit the area in which reflection on failure can take place. The first difficulty arises out of the complex relationships which exist between failure, in its different forms, and fault. The disassociation is all the more delicate and all the more necessary because failure, in certain cases, is a kind of prolongation of fault which it is trying to reveal to consciousness. As real as these relationships are, they must not suggest an assimilation of failure to fault. Nevertheless, it is rare for consciousness, faced with the experience of failure, not to experience a feeling analogous to that which accompanies fault. Faced with the consequences of its action, it is troubled. Failure imposes a kind of interdiction on its undertaking. What seemed possible and was not obtained is considered forbidden. Consciousness reproaches itself, not only for not having outwitted chance, but for having hoped for and desired the very thing which escapes it. Consciousness condemns its presumption if not its imprudence or its inattention. It refuses to consider the consequences of its decision as events which depend on the order of the world and are outside its judgment. It is inclined to trace back to the will the initial and total responsibility for the consequences. When consciousness does not accuse itself of having transgressed something forbidden, it sees in its own initiative the sign of a desire or aspiration which it should have rejected and overcome. Even when it is a question of ends and undertakings which do not directly concern morality, failure manifests itself to consciousness as sanction of transgression. It is transgression of the order of things or of a commandment it misunderstood or of which it was unaware and which failure disclosed to it. Because consciousness suffers from it, it does not consider failure an event but a sanction. Thus failure reinforces the feeling of fault and sometimes creates it. In this way it suggests an interpretation inspired by the idea of a moral or religious law which was forgotten or misunderstood. It is not an easy thing for consciousness to disassociate what belongs to failure from what belongs to fault.

The same conclusion seems to follow if one examines the influence of success on minds which experience it and which have some difficulty keeping themselves from thinking that a cause cannot have been radically bad or censurable which has been victorious in human competition. In the victor himself success tends to recreate a good conscience, to silence scruples, all the more because things and others show themselves docile before the fact and seem to ratify what he has done. What neither pleading nor forces involved in the effort were able to do, success obtained. It rallied human spirits, it seemed in accord with a deep order which would not tolerate that some undertaking would succeed which transgressed fundamental laws of consciousness and of being.

On the other hand, it is certain that, the more consciousness becomes attentive not only to the interiority of its intention or to the quality of its motivation but also to the consequences of its decisions, the more consciousness also abhors disassociating the intrinsic morality of its choices from the consequences which they produce in the world, even though it was difficult to foresee these consequences at the moment of the act. The interference of a multiplicity of factors, whether or not they have moral significance, often gives the act, originally approved by consciousness, an importance which astonishes or infuriates consciousness and seems to some extent to involve its responsibility. Even when the failure of some initiative is properly explained by causes outside the power of the will, it is sufficient that this initiative had initially a moral character for consciousness to be inclined to trace responsibility for the consequences back to its inner act and not to differentiate between failure and fault. Undoubtedly it is true that these causes or conditions in many cases are directly or indirectly dependent on the will. This is so much the case that consciousness has only to follow its natural bent to substitute, for reflection on failure, the avowal of its guilt or a search for responsibility. The primacy of moral causality is opposed to the recognition of failure and distracts reflection from considering independently a problem which, as far as the relationships between value and being are concerned, is as important as the problem of fault. In fact, it covers the whole field of these relationships. Strictly speaking, sovereignly independent morality cannot, in its self-judgment, take into account the way in which the world and other minds welcome it. Failure, on the other hand, redirects our attention to the characteristic of all value to be fully itself only if it is efficacious, if it is ratified in some way by the real, if its expansion in the world is not always opposed or denied. The more that moral values are concentrated in the formal intention of willing or are detached from this willing and constituted as essences, the more do they require reflection to understand the meaning of the failure which moral values seem to experience when the will, using them as rules, tries to incarnate them in the real.

No matter how diverse the forms of failure are, what one seems to find in all of them is a weakness in the relationship of an idea to the concrete existence which this idea attempted to attain, to preserve, or to increase. The possibility of failure arises, it seems, as soon as an idea has a pretension to existence, a pretension to be recognized by minds, a pretension to a certain duration or to a certain diffusion. Even from this point of view, the understanding of failure is not easy. For a judgment able to go beyond appearances, certain types of success will be failures, since they have their origin in ideas which should not succeed. In general, failure often begins well before the time a less acute judgment would customarily place it. There is a certain agreement between the quality of an idea and the kind of success which it can aim at. Nevertheless, it remains true that the question of failure seems to come up each time the expected development or diffusion is lacking for some idea. It also comes up each time the idea incarnating itself in the real produces consequences which appear to be its undoing. Failure is distinguished from fault in this way. According to all appearances, failure involves a synthetic relationship between the idea and the real in which it unfolds. It is necessary for the idea to venture out of itself, to take on flesh in an order where resistance must be overcome. It must institute its own order in that order. If the idea does not succeed in doing so, if it experiences a kind of degradation, one will judge that failure has taken place. One will make the same judgment if the idea effects consequences which turn against it or if, for example, the idea weakens beliefs or institutions which it should, on the contrary, renovate.

However, does it not then follow that failure is necessarily involved in a conception of the realization of ideas which asks from the real only that it present itself as matter to be informed by pre-established finality? An instrumental or technical representation of success and failure, if transposed to moral ideas, either makes ideas appear retrospectively as utopias or condemns them to obtaining successes which are really failures. They are failures in the sense that, far from responding to the intrinsic exigencies of the idea, they change its meaning and denature it. Thus socialist ideas, or some other idea of communitarian society, can be incarnated by institutions which at first will be judged successes but which very soon show themselves to be failures as soon as it becomes evident that they only cover up and even sometimes exacerbate feelings or inclinations whose transformation was the task of the idea. Perhaps there is no failure more serious than that which brings with it the hypocrisy demanded of people when they will not give up ideas which they have traditionally espoused nor the institutions which were to bring about the fulfillment of those ideas. Then institutions are simply excuses for refusing the only changes which could truly maintain the efficaciousness and value of such ideas.

It is to be feared that, in posing the question of failure from the point of view of adequacy between an idea and its realization, one will never escape the judgment of failure. An idea insinuates itself between the interior act that generates it and the concrete change through which one might be able to verify the authenticity of this act. This idea risks falsifying radically our perspective and even forbidding us all reflection on failure. It is a sort of pause in the progress from the interior act to the promotion of existence. It designs a kind of program which seems to us pregnant with action and which hides the idea itself as aborted and incomplete action. Measured by the idea, action will not only not be equal to it but will produce a growing distance between the ambition in the idea and the fact. Breaking away from the interior act from which it issues, and which it appropriates, the idea seems to be self-sufficient and to command from on high the real from which it demands self-confirmation. By separating itself from the act and posing itself in itself, the idea creates between itself and all concrete verification a gulf which can no longer be crossed. All enrichment of the idea and all its promise only underline more emphatically the imperfection of the realization and the kind of betrayal it represents. To discover the source of failure, one must return to the point where the idea, having usurped the place of the interior act to which it is nevertheless indebted for its entire substance, seems in some way superior to the realization which it announces and all of whose value it already contains in advance. Preceding this realization, the idea seems to be master of its conditions. In reality, it experiences failure, which radically questions all the value which it pretended to contain. Thus ideas displace ideas, occasioning each time a kind of mirage of realization, giving rise to the same disappointment.

Certainly, beneath the idea there is a more secret and more intimate act. However, when this idea is nothing more than discourse about the act, it projects a troublesome anticipation of its efficacy, one that is full of trouble because of the kind of disassociation it establishes between a wholly ideal possibility and its realization. Only one change was effected, namely, the creation of a sign. A relationship between future development and an idea, which has already exhausted the strength of the act which is its source, is substituted for the true link between the interior act and the promotion of existence.

Undoubtedly, we must not confuse the idea we have just discussed with the idea which, disengaging itself from development of being, maintains and conserves the inspiration of that development. This kind of idea, in order to better control our future, gives greater depth to the meaning of interior acts and makes an inexhaustible schema for new operations. There is a great difference between an idea which corresponds to a kind of abortion of the act and an idea which gathers in and unifies all the fecundity of a real promotion of our being. However, movement from the second kind of idea to the first begins to be felt as soon as the idea no longer sticks to its task of unifying an interior act and a change which was its expression. When the idea is not isolated from the indivisible unity of an act of consciousness and operation, when it is a reflection of this unity on itself in which the authenticity of the concrete development of being can be appreciated and judged, it does not so much precede the promotion of existence as it illuminates the intuition which we can have of it. But when it sets itself up outside this intuition, it seeks a verification which it can never find. When the act, instead of grasping and understanding itself within the operation in which it unfolds, settles into an idea which subsequently must know realization, it opens the door to failure. This is the other side of a deeper necessity which requires that no advance or true promotion of existence may be preceded by its own idea.

It is not that the act is blind. But the inner light which illuminates it must, before returning to itself, be reflected on the completed operation, on a real transformation of being. If all is restricted to a sign, the unlimited development of signs and the advent of existence are then only two parallel lines. Our astonishment has no other explanation when we must admit that the succession of signs in which humanity dreams or poetizes its history does not correspond to its real history.

In the most favorable instances, when the idea which involves and binds us represents the interim between moments in which the promotion of existence is realized, it is still necessary that a new act make us in some way contemporaneous with the act from which the idea issued. Nothing can ever excuse us, not so much from imitating the idea as from recreating it for the purpose of a new act. This is why the most fruitful ideas, those most capable of diminishing failure, are those which have never finished exhausting the meaning of certain actions which opened up a new history for man and in which we see this union of act and of development, this advance of being, culminate. Meditation on these ideas, by restoring to these operations an actuality impervious to forgetfulness, blocks failure as long as these ideas do not give way to an ideal without force or strength. Lachelier thought he saw a "kind of contradiction between the liberty with which each of us conceives an ideal and works to realize it and the fatality which draws all things around us, even, finally, our own thoughts, far from this ideal" (*Lettres,* p. 114).[1] There is always reason to fear that the ideal is only a dream without any substance if it sets itself up outside the promotion of existence which it illuminates in relationship to its act.

Reflection on failure brings us now to the problem of the idea

1. [*Oeuvres de Jules Lachelier* (Paris: Alcan, 1933).]

in its relationship to being. If being is in the idea, if being is first of all thought, the operation in which it unfolds can add nothing essential to it. It supposes a kind of contact between the idea and matter to which thought knows it is a stranger. There is the seed of an instrumental interpretation of success and failure in this conception. The contradiction pointed out by Lachelier would then be rather an invitation to remain within a life of pure thought. In this perspective, how can one be surprised that an ideal would not, in most cases, succeed in rallying the aid of forces and conditions necessary to it? How could failure really affect ideas? Their value could not be lessened if they are complete in themselves. It is otherwise if the advance of being, which is one with the experience of being, is a creation in which only through reflection can one separate the promotion of existence, the act which engenders it, and the idea which illuminates it. Such advance of being involves a change, be it outwardly visible or invisible. It would not necessarily be a change of movements perceptible to the senses. It is always a regrouping, a concentration, of the energies of being. The productivity which effects the act orders the representation to the self in an instrumental way. In its action it can only grasp the representation as other than the self. The idea is not so much a guide, then, of this operation as it is the way in which it illuminates itself in order to answer for itself.

We can already discern, even within the advance or progress of existence, the presence of a negative element without which this advance would in some way be dissipated in the consciousness of an activity returning unceasingly to itself, exempt from all expansion and from all effort. Just like the experience of fault, the experience of failure stands out against the background of a fundamental experience which it specifies and determines and which accompanies all intuition of existence, even the fullest. Also, just like the experience of fault, the experience of failure could not be what it is if it was not entirely compensated for, and commanded by, a certitude without common measure with the conditions in which for us the promotion of existence takes place. The effort against failure draws its *raison d'être* from an affirmation which is beyond success and failure. It is an affirmation, however, which we would readily betray if we did not actually have to take possession of it, if we were not bound to verify it within operations in which existence progresses. This effort does not at all seek to abolish the fundamental experience of negativity, which stimulates it unceasingly by means of the menace which it holds over us. It seeks to keep what is radically negative in this experience from obtaining predominance in the failure itself. This is why, as also in fault, we assume this experience so that it may incite us to reverse its own meaning and instruct us in operations in which we do not so much succeed in eliminating it as in making it a moment in the progress of existence.

Reflection on failure cannot reveal to us, little by little, the elements of this progress without involving itself in a liberation of the self. It does so by guiding it away from representations of failure which fundamentally misunderstand the relationship which failure has to the essential interests of consciousness and its desire to be. The human spirit easily slips into assuming the same attitude vis-à-vis failure which human understanding might take vis-à-vis phenomena falling under the categories of an object. It allows itself to be overcome by acceptance of an objective failure such as again and again throughout history seems to affect those beliefs which sustain human hope. Initially the self measures the inequality of its being with itself, in which all its failure is found, by the triumph or apparent failure of ideas to which it is devoted, of causes which it defends, and of undertakings in which it is involved. It is right and it is necessary that this should be so. But it is so in order that consciousness may return to itself and that it may make of the deepening of its experience both a way of access to its true causality and a regrasping of self.

The understanding of one's own failure must coincide for the self with the discovery of characteristics of its causality which made failure possible but which can be attained by reflection only insofar as they appear at one and the same time to exclude total failure and to contain a promise of reconciliation and of hope. Besides, would the most obscure consciousness of failure be produced if the characteristics of the causality of the self which reflection will reveal were not involved? What reflection first of all rejects is the idea that a sort of inversion of the causality of the self, in its most normal exercise, would be sufficient to produce the experience of failure. If there is no creative causality which can operate without undergoing some diminution, if there is in any operation an invincible contrariety between the act which promotes existence and the form in which it establishes and defines itself, if the passage from the act, in the impulse which produces it, to its expression includes a kind of pause which has every inspiration standing against itself, then the understanding of failure requires nothing more than the discovery of a law which affects all creative causality. For the self its failure would reside in the perception of a kind of distance between its initial intention and the action which seems to imprison the causality from which it issues. But consciousness must admit that action is accompanied by a most happy surprise. Action purges consciousness of its dreams, it reacts on its author, who receives more than he gave to it of himself. The self could not be satisfied with such understanding of its failure unless there were, at the original moment of invention, a causality which, before offering and diffusing itself, embraced the totality and the fullness of its action. This totality it will only divide and weaken when it encounters and engenders time, space, materiality. The form in which an inspiration would be determined would become its own antagonist: causality could be fruitful only by witholding something of itself and of its original integrity.

If understanding of failure is not to be hindered from the very start, it is necessary to consider that the action in which an interior act is involved is not a debasement of the act but is the only way in which the self can be assured of the content and the meaning of its causality. Neither the matter with which the action seems to be burdened and which seems to deaden its *élan*, nor the definite form which it assumes or designs can be taken as indications of failure for the self. Nevertheless, it is indeed by acting that the self can begin to grasp that its own causality in its greatest intimacy becomes efficacious and real only by making manifest what in itself witnesses not to its subordination to, but to its link with, an obscure foundation, with a mode of being of its being which one would call nature if this word did not immediately connote object. It is in this sense that reflection on self, whose causality has an obligation to action, reveals what no foresight could. It reveals the unfailing presence in the causality of the self, not of a rival causality nor of a force whose influence one might determine, but of a nonbeing which eludes analysis and remains the index of what in the self escapes its power. Nevertheless, this would in no way allow the experience of failure to see clearly into itself if reflection on causality, which it strives to appropriate, did not imply at the same time a pure attention to oneself, capable of grasping the difference between a causality perfectly self-transparent and our real causality. This pure attention is the way a pure consciousness manifests itself. Reflection directs itself toward this pure consciousness which is immanent in its progress.

The concrete forms of the experience of failure, no matter how distant they seem from the discovery of this difference between our real causality and a self-transparent causality, nevertheless take on all their meaning only through this fundamental experience. What is found in all concrete forms of the experience of failure, because of the twofold relationship which causality of self has to a pure intention which illuminates it and to nature, which it bears in itself, is the unexpected predominance of nature. This is true whether these experiences of failure present themselves as the consciousness of possibilities of action, expansion, and love which the self has not exploited, or as the experience of the inequality of the self with itself in any action in which it anticipated this equality, or as a limit encountered in the development of communication, or as the feeling of impurity which is mixed in with the best decisions, or as a subtle betrayal of the beliefs which we profess.

Thus, there seems to be in the recognition of failure something like the conversion of the self as principle of its being. Interrogation of failure begins with an act of divestment in which the self renounces all that it has borrowed and thrusts away the lie of embellishment which all culture occasions. Apart from ordinary experience it can be led to this by the brusque contrast which erupts between its action and the idea which it had of itself. Perhaps when the self no longer fears having been too inferior to its possibilities of being it becomes sensitive to an experience which more emotional forms of failure hid from it. The moment consciousness believes it is entering an entirely luminous region, it notices that its own action has contributed to reconstituting an area of shadow. This is why it is so important for the self to free itself from the illusion that its experience of failure is a passing and relative experience. As long as the tragic in existence is not attenuated, as long as opposition and struggle remain in the foreground and minds experience separation, failure will not attain the fullness of its meaning. In the end, the full meaning of failure will appear only when the self no longer has the feeling of having remained inferior to its deepest possibilities.

As long as consciousness limits itself to measuring failure by the distance between anticipated ends and realized ends, the principal obstacle to reflection on self is the renewal of failure on the historical level. It is not that the distance should not attract our attention. But if consciousness stops there, either it will conceive of an arithmetical growth of its successes capable of suppressing failure or indeed it will turn away from action to seek in a kind of withdrawal into self the way to escape failure. However, it is at the summit of satisfaction, when there is no longer any apparent separation between willing and its accomplishment, that a failure is indicated whose condition is precisely that one cannot confuse it with the forms of failure dependent on impotency, on obstacles to being, and on interruption of the ends of the self. The more intense the certitude which the self has of having enriched and realized its own being in action, the more astonishing is the discovery that it makes of a relationship which had to elude it as long as its attention was on the work to be done. Consciousness manifests itself to itself as mediator between operations requiring multiple collaboration borrowed from the order of the world and an aspiration which is radically of another order. As long as it concentrated its effort in action, the self always felt that, in renouncing itself for action, it increased its chances of realizing itself. This is indeed what happens. However, the very authenticity of this success, by fulfilling directly the hopes of consciousness, also gives it insight into a relationship between the satisfaction of the self linked to the accomplished work and a deeper desire coming from another source. The feeling of disappointment, which always goes with satisfaction and which does not so much depreciate it as give it a new dimension, is the index of a desire embodied in determined goals but never exhausted by these goals and their success. Even if action is disappointing, consciousness cannot overlook it in order to be equal to itself, for action hides from the self its true being as much as it reveals it. The puzzlement of consciousness that results is occasioned by the duality of aspects found in any experience. On the one hand, there is a growth of value for the self, and, on the other, there is awareness of an ever resurging difference between the self and its being. The deepening of reflection attains its full significance after one has eliminated all forms of failure which consciousness might suspect as being simply the continuation of fault, akin to the complications of the moral world and to inner conflicts, or dependent on conditions which would indeed make success difficult or improbable but not really impossible.

This disappointment, which appears on the fringes of a fulfilled consciousness, is promptly differentiated by the self from the kind of failure which reveals resistance to its expansion. The self is puzzled by it and does not know what to make of it until it discovers, through its impotency to remain in possession, that it cannot force access to its own being except with a militant freedom. But it also discovers that this militant freedom is the aspect which a consciousness dependent on the world and on nature takes on in its relationship to a pure affirmation of self, superior to all nature. It is in moments when man desires nothing other than the satisfaction which comes to him through ends he envisioned or because of decisions he has taken, it is in moments when the world, no less than other minds, responds to his wishes, that a failure can unambiguously reveal itself which cannot be ascribed to contingent conditions or to weak effort but to the very structure of the self, to the constant tensions and mutual attractions among the relationships constituting its being. In order to free itself completely from all fallacious hope as well as from all pessimism, consciousness seeks to prolong reflection begun by meditation on failure and to return to the very principle without which, certainly, there would be no question of either success or failure. This ground is beyond both and is never touched by them, even though it is the foundation of our judgment about them and the rule for our striving.

In any case, the immediate benefit of a deepening of the experience which the self makes of its own failure is to make henceforth impossible an entirely objective view of failure which one might call objective and which concerns the destiny of human effort considered in its totality and in its particular moral and cultural accomplishments. It also keeps an entirely impersonal ascertainment of the failure of human ambitions on the historical plane from influencing consciousness and depressing it. If the self cannot reflect on the possibility of an authentic experience of failure without discovering the secret of its hope and strength, it also verifies that beneath the objective failure, which one believes one can examine without taking into account operations of consciousness, one can find the same relationships to a liberty which cannot abdicate in favor of ideas or institutions claiming an independent life without radically falsifying the meaning of failure. Ideas neither live nor die without the aid, the abstention, or the forgetfulness of consciousness. Aside from the fact that one often attaches the value of an experience to what was only a succession of events on which one hung ideas, the apparent impersonality of historical becoming, worked over and oriented by ideas, must not hide the actions and the incessant operations which constitute it. The degeneration of the idea, the degradation of value which accompanies it, its impotency to shape the real, in which we see a sign of failure, cannot be separated from the concrete acts by which the most intimate movements of the human spirit measure their value. Constitutions collapse, institutions disappear, civilizations become nothing but décor, and one thinks that it is a sign of failure for the ideas whose expression they wanted to be. But for a long time ideas were already detached from living minds and had passed into the state of signs. It is not nature which in the end necessarily wins out over the demands of consciousness. The conditions of possibility of an experience of failure and of reflection on failure elude us on the historical level itself, as soon as we isolate the relationship between ideas, or ideals, and the real from the interior act in which the relationship recreates itself. For this reason, we are often led to consider as failures experiences which attest to the fact that the very conditions of failure were lacking, namely, the operations in which the act as generative of an idea can judge of its value by the concrete change in which it reflects itself because it contrived to produce it. True failure is only too real, but it is truly failure only to the extent that the reflection which appropriates it discerns its double relationship to freedom and to a nature in which freedom must involve itself in order to judge both itself and the idea immanent in its operation. The contrast between reality and the ideals in which man dreams his future or that of society would not puzzle consciousness so much if it consented to return to itself thanks to failure itself. It prefers to impute either to ideas or to nature a failure in which it should discern only the absence of conditions which would give failure authentic meaning and fecundity. Where there is no true test, one will speak of failure; one will then go from a moral and social idealism, which one believes one has outgrown, to a social pessimism and realism. Art, the novel, all of culture contribute to an accentuation and a masking of this disaccord between ideas and the stuff of being. The artist rids himself of his dreams by creating characters out of them. This way he acquires sanity for himself. But the characters live in the consciousness of other men whose real history receives the addition of fanciful creation with which they no longer know how to equate their action. Culture, in its totality, gives man an idea of self which lifts him far above the animal kingdom but which does not reach his real being. This inequality, this dissymmetry, between man as he is in the works which he adds to nature and as he is in his authentic being, could be the starting point for reflection on failure. It would keep consciousness from assimilating the being of man to the being that creates culture. However, once man has given himself language, signs, and symbols which he can fulfill and change indefinitely, man has given himself at the same time the means with which to trick himself. His works change him less than they change the signs in which he believes he recognizes himself. Thus is created a kind of mirage, which disappears suddenly when it is necessary for the self to tear itself away from itself to create itself in an operation in which its own act and its being are but one. This is why reflection on failure begins in all cases with an act of renunciation which delivers us, not from failure, but from the forgetting of failure and from the illusions which hide it from us.

3 / The Deepening of Solitude

THE EXPERIENCE OF FAULT, even though at first it has a merely moral character, gives access in reflection to a metaphysical experience which confers on it a new meaning at the level of action. In like manner, concrete relations among minds which respond to the demands of the moral law within communities and groups would not have all their depth if they did not depend on an experience of solitude. At first they set out to occasion solitude, but, in deepening itself, solitude gives them a richness which in any other case they would not have had. When interpersonal relations have a specifically moral character, they make us desire and call for, as much as they already presuppose, minds capable of saying "we" and of breaking the bounds of individuality. However, only minds which have experienced solitude can truly say "we" and can consider moral relations which bind them to other beings as the beginning, the means, and the preparation for a deeper friendship which has its guarantee in the certitudes which solitude allowed one to attain. The order of dutiful relations would not involve the highest interests of consciousness to such a degree if it did not present an order of relations in which a unitive life was verified which reasonably might be hoped for only by minds to whom solitude had revealed their true being. Among the communities in which the moral effort of humanity is distributed, it would be difficult to find a single one which, by means of the common pursuit of ends and the strengthening of bonds between individuals, did not have in mind a deeper unitive life, the desire for which can only arise in minds awakened to themselves by solitude.

Exchange among minds is of necessity begun in complete ignorance of both the conditions which make it possible and the consequences which it has for the coming-to-be of each self. A consciousness which expects or obtains responses, promises, and signs of friendship and love from another consciousness does not know what it owes to these responses in being able to take possession of itself and of its own interiority. Nor does it doubt that it exists for the other consciousness just as the other consciousness exists for it. That a consciousness which gives me orders or which responds to my appeal would be reduced to a group of representations and that, in parallel fashion, my existence would be reduced for this consciousness to a group of representations is an idea which is simply inconceivable as long as I do not substitute for the actuality of communication a problem which arises out of the relationship between a knowing subject and the world. Here we have a first fundamental given which mere speculative reflection never succeeds in reducing and which keeps us from considering the actuality of the existence of minds, one for the other, using the model of the actuality of the existence of an object for a subject. It is the reciprocity of their acts which is primary and which awakens each consciousness to itself before subjecting and directing its development at all times.

The feeling of solitude in its most primitive and rudimentary form is born out of the interruption of these acts. This interruption creates something like a lacuna in the consciousness of our being. We are not surprised so much by being left once again to ourselves as we are of being suddenly deprived of a possibility of being which seemed properly to belong to us. Also, the intermittence of acts of communication first plunges consciousness into a kind of dream. Such a consciousness does not so much seek its way toward itself as in some way it goes to sleep, since it no longer needs to be vigilant, as reciprocal acts of appeal and response required. This consciousness no longer has to raise itself to the level of communication, but it is still impotent to make of its solitude a way of access to its own being. It might rather be tempted to settle down in its dream and forget what it owes to communication, withdrawing into what it believes to be the self but which is only an incomplete and almost cocoon-like life. The breakup of the moral world in all its forms has its origin in the danger which solitude brings about when, instead of being the starting point for a deepening of self, it suggests to consciousness that it might be self-sufficient.

The response of communication makes this dream evaporate. However, in another way, the self comes willingly to adopt the idea that solitude simply translates the desire for a reciprocity momentarily suspended, that it is nothing more than the disappointment produced by this interruption of communication. Peopled by memories of presence and encounter with other minds, solitude seems to identify with nostalgia for an interrupted experience.

Nevertheless, it is not in vain that the intermittence of reciprocal acts occasioned the feeling of solitude. This feeling infiltrates and insinuates itself as apprehension or as fear when the exchange between minds is restored. It gives birth to the suspicion that communication is neither sufficiently true nor sufficiently deep to overcome the separation of minds; it introduces something like a new dimension into communication. The feeling of solitude cannot be reduced to an echo of communication, no matter how ignorant it still is concerning itself. It evokes a movement of reflection from which consciousness senses that it will come out stronger and more assured of itself in returning to communication. It is able to give communication its full measure and to keep it from becoming a dissipation for the self. Once the feeling of solitude acquires sufficient intensity to produce disappointment and distress for consciousness, it can no longer agree to see in communication alone the way to appease itself and perhaps to deceive itself. Solitude seeks to understand itself; or rather, consciousness, relying on solitude, seeks to discover a certitude which could well illuminate communication but which would not be dependent on it. Solitude suggests to the self that, alone before itself, the self is no less separated from itself than it is from other minds in communication. It also suggests that the *raison d'être* of this separation is identical in both instances, just as the certitude which permits us to overcome it is also identical in both instances.

Renouncing for a moment the satisfaction given by communication to its need for security, the self cannot turn toward itself without experiencing in a most vivid way the link between its feeling of solitude and the contingency of its being. Since consciousness drew its experience of self first of all from communication, since it borrowed from communication its feeling of existence, the moment it tries to take possession of itself independently from communication, consciousness cannot help feeling suddenly powerless to sustain itself; it cannot help having a painful feeling of solitude. Will it hasten to ask communication again for some way of breaking this solitude, or will it have the courage to give it depth? It is necessary then for the self to agree to abandon fallacious guarantees it received from communication. It must put aside, one after the other, all the forms embraced by it in its relations with other minds. It is necessary for it to cease speaking to itself as a being capable of communication and as it does in communication. It must give up all dialogue with itself in which it interiorly prolongs its conversation with other minds. It must undertake to go toward itself without this dialogue and without the additional existence which it owes to it. If the self decides to go all the way in this self-deprivation, which it began in order to dig deeper into the subjectivity which eludes it, in order to force its secret with the aid of the feeling of solitude; if the self divests itself of everything that does not properly belong to it, everything which it risks being deprived of at any moment and which one day it will inevitably lose, everything that it has appropriated and which seems to be part of its substance; if the self removes from its feeling of existence and from its experience of being the memories and the testimonies of love and the self-enrichment it owes to its familiarity with great human enterprises; if it does all these things, the self immediately falls back into a subjectivity whose origin and *raison d'être* radically escape it.

Nevertheless, the feeling of solitude has been profoundly changed by the very movement of this ascesis. In the beginning it was the experience of privation of being by the interruption of the communication of minds. Deepened by a consciousness which turned toward itself, renouncing all privileges which veiled its being, solitude became the experience of an impoverishment whose depths the self believes it touches after it has ejected from itself all that it borrowed from communication. Why is it at this moment, when all communication is lacking, that the self senses in the experience of its impoverishment a certitude which rescues it from solitude in quite a different way than did the communication of minds? It is because the self discovers that this operation, in which it gives up all it believed belonged to it, could not have been accomplished, or even suggested, unless it was done by an act of pure consciousness of self. The self is unceasingly joined to this act of pure consciousness just as much as it is joined to a foundation of given existence which it cannot reduce. Reflection on fault involves the beginning of regeneration, whose source is in the relationship of the reflecting self to the principle by which it is judged more than it judges itself. Likewise, the deepening of solitude, having retreated from intermittent or disappointing communication, intensifies the experience of our impoverishment only to allow us to find in it the assurance of help which cannot betray us. If we were not absolutely a being other than the one we find in ourselves when we are deprived, or when we deprive ourselves, of the comfort of communication, the feeling of our impoverishment would be unintelligible to us. This deeper awareness of solitude could not happen except through an action in us of something which wholly transcends us. Only that self is capable of solitude which, having renounced all that made it consider itself as a being among other beings, would cease to be for itself. This would not be possible unless its consciousness of self were effected by an act which absolutely transcends it as self. Thus, the deepening of solitude, just as reflection on fault or failure, coincides with the beginning of self-regeneration.

The surest sign of this regeneration is the change in our feeling of solitude within communication. The discontinuities of acts of self-attention have nothing in common with the interruptions or the intermittences in a recurrently broken dialogue. The actuality of the certitude obtained by reflection on solitude is not subject to the vicissitudes of the communication of minds. Thus, communication can become a trial which in certain cases intensifies or exacerbates the feeling of solitude. Nevertheless, it does so in such a way that the self never doubts that the obstacles to communication of minds are to be found in the overlooking of true being, which they discovered, or could discover, in the depths of solitude. Minds withdraw, they hide from one another, as if they wished to guard in themselves contingency and nothingness. If the self finds no echo, no response to its appeal, certainly it experiences a feeling of solitude, but it will have transcended the stage in which it was astonished by, and suffered from, being alone. The memory of the happiness of communication, joined to the certitude of the principle which is at the root of its being, will aid and sustain it in the hours of abandonment. On the other hand, self-depreciation of what is contingent in it does not induce it to depreciate individual differences in other minds with which it communicates. On the contrary, it sees that these differences make communication moving and precious, make it fragile but also cooperate to give it depth. It is no paradox to think that we must first of all eliminate in ourselves the difference in the operation by which we truly enter into possession of our being and recognize this question in another, hoping that it remains the resistance, the means through which a communication will be created whose intimacy does not contradict its liberating character. We cannot effectively verify and experience the value of the act by which we have asked solitude for the secret of our being except by loving other selves with respect to that which makes them other than us. No consciousness can feel itself loved, even in that which kept it initially from fleeing from its given being, without becoming free in relation to this being. No longer is there for it something like the fatality of solitude. The secret sorrow of an unloved being comes from the feeling that without love it cannot be freed of itself. Undoubtedly, disappointments remain linked to the experience of communication. But in the end they have their full meaning only for a consciousness which, having renounced selflessly all that is individual in its being, opened itself to communication. When communication attains a certain degree of depth, it reveals to each consciousness the sweetness of a feeling witnessing to the fact that the defenses with which the individual self thought it had to protect itself have been broken.

Solitude evokes communication, excites desire for it. However, solitude is not overcome by a communication which surpasses in dignity and constancy all the precarious and incomplete communications accorded to us. When one opposes solitude to communication in this manner, one still leaves solitude in a relative stance. One introduces communication, or the memory of communication, into solitude, but it is a communication which one knows to be menaced or which one endangers so as to distinguish it from a communication in which consciousness unfolds. The incessant passage from solitude to communication is then only the passage from incomplete or unhappy communication to communication which momentarily appeases desire. One should understand the relationship between solitude and communication otherwise. A solitude which is not relative but absolute is the ferment and never rejected condition in communication. It is that solitude which consciousness attains when it forgoes all it is accustomed to consider its own but which belongs to it only because of its interchange with other minds. This solitude is not entirely absent from even the most fulfilled communication. It is much truer to say that communication is created and enriched by it alone, even while it fights against it. In the happiest communication there persists the menace of less successful communication. This menace is the way solitude makes itself felt within communication. Undoubtedly, we must agree that communication saves one from solitude but only in the sense that it confirms its presence at the very instant it triumphs over it.

However, how can communication, in this entirely relative sense, save us from solitude if it does not include a certitude, an assurance of another order which does not cease to be present to it and which is such that no disappointment, no separation, or, for that matter, no satisfaction is large enough to keep a consciousness from always turning toward others, seeking dialogue with them? What is absolute failure for solitude, or rather what is revealed only in solitude and in the deepening of self to which it invites us, is not communication but what has to be superior to all communication. It then becomes immanent in each of the forms of communication, always requiring of communication more than it will be capable of giving. Communication cannot truly unite selves unless each of them is allowed for itself to understand both the solitude to which it is condemned by what is contingent and given in it and the principle of unity which makes it capable of love. Between the moment in which we are invited to go toward ourselves, starting with a spontaneously realized communication, and the moment in which we freely seek communication, is located the deepening of a solitude in which consciousness discovers what transcends communication but which also makes communication incomplete and yet always rich with promise.

At the same time, from this point of view, one can understand how the desire is born for communication which would transcend the conditions in which, here below, the dialogue of minds takes place. It is a desire for communication not based on reciprocal relations of two causalities, each of which remains uncertain of the inner and secret act of the other. It is a desire for communication based on the actuality of absolute communication and on the presence of a consciousness all of whose appeals are heard and from which nothing is hidden of those things which men hide from one another as well as from themselves. It would be a communication which, going to the depths of being which we ignore, would also give us the assurance that on us alone, because its love is inexhaustible, definitely depends the possibility of emptying out our solitude. Not only would all other forms of communication fade in the presence of this highest communication, but the very idea of communication would change meaning and value, as would the idea of solitude.

Likewise, once communication is defined as a relation between minds, each of whose being, in its greatest intimacy, is not created by the act of communication but exists prior to it, the task of communication seems to be to break a solitude indebted to the fact that each consciousness, existing first of all for itself, is capable of a gift of self, just as it is capable of promises, without ceasing to be in some way a unity or a being among other beings. Solitude is then a primary fact. But it seems one is closer to experience if one sees communication as the primary fact from which is born the feeling of existence for self and also, because of reflection, solitude. Solitude does not at all coincide with consciousness of *ego*. On the contrary, it is that which consciousness, born of communication, comes up against when it is deprived of communication. When consciousness meditates on its solitude and deepens it, it will grasp within its desire for new communication much more than the desire to find again the experience of self. It will see in communication not only the way for self to exist but the verification of a certitude of unity whose negation solitude properly is. Between solitude, which presents itself as more radical than it probably really is, and the certitude of pure consciousness of self, communication, at all levels, produces an experience of self which is removed from all categories by which the relation between two separated beings can be represented. Within nostalgia for an impossible unity and in the hopeless desire to absolutely escape solitude, minds give to one another possession of self.

One can already find in communication and in solitude understood in this way strong reasons for not confusing the principle toward which a consciousness deepening its experience of solitude directs itself and the principle which, from another point of view, one can judge as required for understanding that there are not so much worlds as there are particular minds. The idea of a plurality of fields of consciousness, involving different contents because of their very plurality, contradicts the unity of a world required by rational thought, as long as one does not find a way for these minds to communicate or rather to establish between themselves relations which order them to an identical universe. A plurality of subjects is presupposed at the origin of communication, no matter how one subsequently conceives it, whether as the fragmentation or the expression of a single center. In any kind of monadology solitude is from the beginning excluded by the fact of the solidarity of minds which expresses the unity of the world. There is no problem of solitude. Solitude can only mean isolation. Further, there is no problem of solitude if, outside the pure subject, which is in charge of the unity of experience, one wishes to recognize only empirical individuality.

The principle which saves us from solitude does not effect the link, does not make the unity of all kinds of communication, in the sense that one might think that it includes them and comprehends all of them. It does not coordinate them the way we conceive the unity of a system or of a totality to be guaranteed. The question can be posed in this manner only for subjects whom one objectifies in some way and of whom one asks immediately how they make up a world, that is, how they are at once dependent and solidary. It is not posed in this way for minds which can be treated numerically only if one has already agreed to consider them from outside. The question is not posed in the same manner for minds which are indebted to their dialogue for the highest concrete experience of self of which they are capable, a dialogue always susceptible of disruption and whose intermittences engender an experience of solitude which is not to be compared to independence with respect to a system. When the exigencies of thought which are at the basis of a monadology mix with reflection on solitude and communication, they denature the meaning of a dialogue which does not take place between subjects, prisoners of a same objective order, but which, on the contrary, creates minds or promotes them to experience of self.

BOOK II
Primary Affirmation

4 / Pure Consciousness

APPROPRIATION OF OUR PAST has opened up an inquiry which must now be continued for itself. This inquiry is to be pursued by withdrawing a little more from history toward a present which is not one of decision directed to the future. It is a present congenial to reflection, where consciousness directs itself toward self-understanding and the possession of a certitude which ought then to become immanent in all ethical regulations. This reflection is a moment in the experience which goes from action in its spontaneity to reflection on action, and from reflection to full consciousness of self, and then returns to goals and to the world.

No matter what differences there are between the experience of fault, failure, and solitude, the feelings which they occasion or which accompany them are sufficiently similar to appear as the expression of a fundamental feeling which translates the inadequacy of ourselves to ourselves or of the being which we become to our true being. Whatever the differences between the analyses we have made of these three experiences, they bring consciousness to a single question.

Why, one might ask, retain from the past only those traits which offer the self a diminished image of its being? Why not choose experiences where the self—in success, in friendship, or in duty—feels equal to itself? This is in effect to ask whether it is necessary for a reflective inquiry to take as its primary givens moments in the life of the self which betray incompleteness in the fulfillment of its desire, even weakness in its willing. However, this necessity is not at all different from that which in the

[41]

theoretical order obliges us to pass through ignorance and error before attaining science. It does not prejudge the later orientation of reflection. It only implies recognition that there is no progress toward self which does not include reflection on experiences which first interest us more for what they offer negatively than for what we can make of their immediate affinity with the profound aspirations of the self. Reflection must judge what is negative in them, and it can do this in different ways, which are so many directions for philosophical thought. But the initial intention of hiding this negative element, of judging it to be illusory, is a willingness to ignore what is most characteristic of human experience and most fruitful for its progress. Besides, one can pretend to recognize it, with the intention, however, of reducing it, of erasing its meaning, of acknowledging its presence just long enough to be aware of the delay in acquisition of knowledge or in progress toward possession which would give consciousness its peace.

Therefore, it is necessary that the experiences offered to reflection be chosen in such a way that they do not allow the problem to be avoided. Nevertheless, is there not something arbitrary in the choice and limitation of experiences which are for us like a text to be interpreted? Certainly one could list other experiences. But one should notice that the experiences of failure, fault, and solitude have common traits which keep us from assimilating them to experiences belonging to other functions of consciousness, the esthetic or the theoretical, for example. In the experiences of failure, fault, and solitude there are three negations of a fundamental ambition, of an identical desire, which does not concern the assimilation of an object by a subject but the generation of a world of relations which would make minds transparent to one another and to themselves. Thus they include a good part of the domain of an ethic. These experiences are evidence of an identical desire. It is quite likely that they include an identical certitude.

One can grasp the importance of the choice of first givens, of first experiences on which reflection must bear. Correlatively, there should be no rule in philosophy more clear than this: not to extend the signification of a principle beyond the experiences which permitted its discovery. The concern to reconcile principles to which reflection exercised on irreducible experiences has led us, the concern not only to reconcile them but to unify them,

to erase their functional diversity, often brings about the consequence that a single principle is invoked to answer fundamentally different questions. There are areas of reflection. If it is true
that reflection is always an effort of consciousness to understand
itself, it follows that a subject corresponds to each of these areas
who does not so much exist prior to reflection as he defines and
constitutes himself by means of it. Even if the subject cannot
complete this self-understanding by himself, as long as he directs himself toward the affirmation of a principle from which
the initiative of reflection itself issues, this principle remains
relative to the experiences which are at the origin of this progress toward consciousness of self. It is in this sense that the
determination of the reflective givens already involves an intention which is like a first act by which the subject, working to
understand himself, molds himself. One can sense that the principle through which the subject of reflection will understand
himself must be immanent, not only in the operations guiding
consciousness toward the principle but also in the experiences
which are at the starting point of the entire reflective search.

There is no surer way for us to determine that the experiences chosen, which could easily be augmented with similar
experiences, constitute an area of reflection than to ask ourselves first of all whether the effort made by consciousness in
using them to understand and define itself coincides with the
effort consciousness realizes in order to constitute itself as subject in other groups of experiences which no one would question
as authentic. A single "Who am I?" must correspond to each area
of reflection. If it is possible for the self to give an answer
identical to the one it gave elsewhere, this would be an indication that the experiences it is now interrogating do not constitute
an independent area of reflection.

If consciousness attempts, from this point of view, to understand itself through failure or fault in the same way that it
understands itself when it grasps itself as the subject of operations which give birth to the universe of knowledge, it must soon
abandon its attempt. Undoubtedly, behind the subject of knowledge, there always is consciousness of an activity which over-
flows all the structures whose presence reflection discerns in
knowledge. Undoubtedly, consciousness, grasping itself as subject, avoids any danger of falling, itself, to the level of a given. It
protects itself against the confusion which could take place be-

tween what it is as individual consciousness and what it is when it exercises its creative power. The initiatives of the subject of knowledge, no matter how contingent they may be, are ranged invincibly within internal necessities, within laws of construction whose validity is a function of the intelligibility which they introduce into the real. Every creation embodies itself, immediately, in a form in which the subject can read reflectively the direction of an effort oriented toward the increase of knowledge and toward the agreement among themselves of human spirits. Certainly, the configuration of the world lends itself to these forms in such an intractable manner that there is always some resistance to be overcome. This resistance, far from awakening in the subject a doubt as to its own fecundity, requires it to loosen, renew, or regroup the forms engaged in knowledge. The element of opposition in this resistance is the indication of what in the real is not constructed by the subject. The subject is not affected by this resistance, and its interiority is comparable to the transparency gained for itself through reflection by an intellectual dynamism whose identity in all subjects is correlative to the unity of the object. If consciousness, in which this intellectual dynamism comes into possession of itself, asks itself what it is, it will answer that it is anonymous, just as the dynamism capable of founding the unity of human spirits and the unity of the object is anonymous. This consciousness does not know what it is to be more or less distant from itself, as is a consciousness which makes itself more or less the accomplice of forces which betray it, which affect it, and to which it remains united.

Could not a consciousness capable of fault and solitude succeed both in understanding itself and understanding what is negative in certain moments of its existence if it grasped itself essentially within thought as a moment of thought? Would it not see in fault, failure, and solitude the consequence and the expression of a limitation which affects thought when it thinks itself in particular and finite minds? From this point of view, is there anything more in failure or in fault than there is in error linked to processes of thought which at first is not at the level of thought or in possession of all being?

Failure, fault, or the experience of solitude would, from this point of view, be the consequence and the affective translation of an original limitation of thought in particular minds. They would be eliminated when consciousness, seeking to understand itself, would recognize its subordination to the actuality of thought in which are concentrated the eternal relations which are the guarantee of its judgments and its internal movements. Just as a judgment, one might say, which freed us from error, is the sign that the conquered truth existed prior to our search and was in a way in itself before being for our thought, which aimed at it without attaining it, so reflection, which delivers us from fault or from solitude, would manifest their partial and illusory character by revealing to us our solidarity with the totality of being and of thought.

Even if it were legitimate from another point of view and for other areas of reflection, this opposition between finite thought and thought coextensive with being would hardly satisfy the requirements of consciousness reflecting on the experiences of fault or of failure, which for it are inseparable from its loss, its salvation, from its chances to be. The privative character of an inadequate thought does not substantially remove it from the totality of thought of which it is a moment and from which it cannot be separated. Just as it is impossible to conceive that the totality of thought would not be present in each thought, the partiality of knowledge and even the apparent multiplicity of centers in which it reflects are only the expression of an obscurity which the progress of knowledge dispels. The affective character which in certain cases is added to the experience of this inadequacy, or the feeling of decadence which can accompany it, only underlines a little more the confusion of relationships; it does not change their nature. The nonbeing of this privation is always relative to a higher degree of clarity and to a fullness of being.

However, we have seen that the nonbeing grasped by reflection in the depths of the experiences of fault and of solitude is not susceptible of being progressively reduced or lessened. There is no translation or symbol of this nonbeing in the language of thought or of categories. Even though nonbeing becomes virulent only through our help or our decision, it slips into our desire to be, or to be worthwhile, as much as into our acts. It mixes with solitude, with communication, with fault, with satisfaction, with failure, with the unfolding of consciousness. If this nonbeing becomes determinate or specific in our decadence or in the joy of communication, it is always entirely there where its presence is felt, that is, in each of the experiences which decide for the self what it is and what it is worth. It is not there more or less, but absolutely, even when our experience of being nears its greatest transparency. This is why this nonbeing, far from identifying itself with the finite character of consciousness, prohibits, on the contrary, an understanding of self to be made through a relation in which we would grasp ourselves in the perspective of an opposition between limited thought and absolute thought. The first result of the deepening of experiences in which nonbeing manifests itself is to direct consciousness away from understanding itself in a relationship in which nonbeing would have only a privative character and would express itself only by predicative opposition bearing on the mode of being of existences which are ranged as contraries in a single genus: finite and infinite, partial and total, particular and universal.

Consciousness will now turn more freely toward the search for certitude—which it has anticipated attaining ever since the dawn of reflection. It could well be that certitude may seem as distant from the experiences which lead toward it as is the very nonbeing whose discovery they permitted. It could also be that this certitude, just like nonbeing, enters into these experiences only by becoming specific and determinate for a concrete consciousness, for a real consciousness, as often and in as many ways as the conditions of the communication of minds or the nature of fault or of failure are modified. What, at first, is most abstract for a consciousness while it lives these experiences is also what is most concrete once it undertakes reflectively to grasp within these experiences the basis for what is disappointing in them as well as for what they contain of hope and of courage. What is abstract in a principle explains why one cannot deduce from it the content of experiences in which it is involved. However, on the other hand, it can be what is most concrete because it is the inner light of these experiences. The certitude which reflection discerns at work within the most concrete willing is abstract with respect to this willing. But, from another point of view, it is highly concrete because it secretly sustains willing, because it regulates it and is not affected by its weaknesses or overwhelmed by its successes. What is most concrete is not what is richest in determinations; it is what orders and saves.

All experiences which involve nothing less for the self than its assurance of being are related to a certitude which cannot pass over into any one of them but which judges them and keeps the self from absolutely despairing of itself at the very moment that it is most distant from itself. This is why all the conceivable mediations and all the steps which one might arrange through a secretly oriented goal can do no more than delay the moment in which the exigency of a mediation [1] excluding all separation between the self and its principle is imposed. The being of the self can only be born from the understanding which it acquires concerning itself by an affirmation which engenders and regenerates it. If there were not reciprocity within this affirmation between the act by which it produces itself and the act by which it is transparent to itself in the kinds of consciousness which affirm it, the self would remain separated from its source.

The act by which I affirm the absolute affirmation is worthless unless it is the absolute affirmation which affirms itself in me and through me and thus guarantees my affirmation and sustains it. The movement by which I raise myself to this affirmation could, consequently, seem illusory. I do not so much progress toward it as I discern it little by little in the depths of my thoughts and my feeings. The moment at which I completely take possession of this affirmation is rather the moment in which it completely takes possession of my consciousness. It does so in such a way, in fact, that there is not so much relationship of my affirmation to the absolute affirmation as efficacy of the absolute affirmation in my affirmation and through my affirmation. Strictly speaking, the initiative of affirmation is wrested from me.

However, if it produces my affirmation, does not the absolute affirmation rob me of the means by which I might guarantee for myself its authenticity? Even more, does it not deprive me of the very thing I asked of it: the certitude of being worthwhile as

1. [There seems to be a misprint in the French. *Méditation* is found where *médiation* seems to be required by the sense of the passage, for the earlier part of the sentence also speaks of *médiation*. However, there is some ambiguity here, for it is precisely the philosophical meditation which is reflective philosophy which is the meditation "excluding all separation between the self and its principle. . . ." This sense is borne out by the next sentence of the paragraph, which reads: "The being of the self can only be born *from the understanding* (my italics) which it acquires concerning itself by an affirmation which engenders and regenerates it."— TRANSLATOR'S NOTE.]

long and as often as I might affirm it? If it makes my affirmation invincible, I do not understand that it sometimes seems to escape me when I lose hold of myself or that it should be present when I get hold of myself.

Might I proceed otherwise? Might I be permitted, if not to submit, at least to link the absolute affirmation to my judgment, to my reflection, even to my resolve not to find inner peace unless I should first be assured that in this peace lives a certitude which surpasses it? Thus I restore a *quid proprium* to my act and a meaning to my effort. Nevertheless, is not this gain obtained under conditions that threaten to wipe it out? Is not the act which is in my judgment now at the source of the absolute affirmation? But if it conditions this absolute affirmation, how can this absolute affirmation still serve as a guarantee or fill my spirit in such a way that the renunciation of all that might come from my act itself may be justified?

I am then led to question, alternately, either my affirmation, if it proceeds from the absolute affirmation, or the absolute affirmation, if it is my judgment which must lead me there. In both cases I must forfeit my certitude. For this certitude is indivisibly certitude of my act of affirmation and, within this act, certitude of any affirmation which no act can exhaust, even though it offers itself entirely to each of them.

However, does not the doubt, which alternately affects one or the other of these certitudes, come from the disassociation which I allow to happen between the act of my reflection or of my judgment and the operation which penetrates, goes beyond, or founds them? When I consent to this disassociation, the feeling is weakened in which I experience that I belong to myself the more I belong entirely to the affirmation which affirms itself in me as I affirm myself through it. Then the abstract question is posed: How can my affirmation take its value from an affirmation which it affirms and which seems then to hold its authority only from the act which affirms it? I cannot, in fact, answer if the affirmation which saves me is not interior to my affirmation to the same degree that my own affirmation is interior to it.

The act of renunciation, by which I absolutely put myself in second place, restores the unity of certitude and cuts through a difficulty raised by theoretical thought which could have led me to conclude differently. The "I am" expresses at once the highest certitude and the renunciation of self which accompanies it. It is simultaneously turned toward itself, whose destiny it hopes henceforth to regulate, and toward the absolute affirmation which it appropriates. It is by the "I am" that the self can subsequently have a history which a certitude unchangeable in its principle dominates and judges. Not that this certitude is always present to consciousness. But one might say that its actuality does not depend on its presence. When consciousness recaptures it and regenerates itself through it, it is nothing but the passage from self-distraction to self-attention.

Still, the twofold relationship which envelops the "I am"— the relationship on the one hand to self, on the other to the absolute affirmation—indeed makes it manifest that the liberation effected by the highest certitude is both absolute and unreal. It is absolute because there is nothing in the "I am" which is susceptible of addition or of increase. It is unreal because the self through which it counts has not yet begun to change or be transformed. If the "I am" expresses the way in which consciousness appropriates the affirmation which saves it, the self, for which the "I am" assumes responsibility, experiences immediately that it can only ask action and effort for a difficult and always incomplete victory over what keeps it from being fully transparent to itself. The absolute affirmation which affirms itself within my affirmation then produces both a certitude and an appeal. The appeal is addressed to the self in order that, in the world and within duration, through duty and, if necessary, through sacrifice, it verify the "I am" and make a reality of it. This certitude is the actuality of a relationship which neither failures nor forgetfulness affect because it is immanence within "I am" of an affirmation which surpasses all multiplicity as well as erases all separation between subjects.

The "I am," far from being the autonomous positioning of a subject, is nothing less than the absolute affirmation affirming itself through the act of a consciousness which becomes consciousness of self at the very moment it discovers that it is not in virtue of itself. There is no question here of a genesis which would restore between the "I am" and its principle a difference of genus such as that between beings. There is absolute inequality between the "I am" and the affirmation which grounds it only on the condition that all relationship which would constitute an obstacle to their reciprocal interiority is ruled out. However, every relationship which postulates some separation between the terms which it links is a relationship of this kind. Either it occasions this separation or unites what was separated or justifies a certain disproportion between beings which it brings together, or it works at ensuring their analogy. On the contrary, the interiority to the "I am" of the ineffable affirmation which it appropriates does not exclude a radical incommensurability. For the "I am" does not make relative to itself the affirmation by which a consciousness becomes consciousness of self. Its act is the avowal of an absolute affirmation which it grasps within this avowal. It is not a judgment; it is the promise of a guarantee for all judgments, for all decisions for which this affirmation will be the soul. Consequently, this affirmation is distinct from all that it will allow us to say, to know, or to do when saying, knowing, and doing have some value. None of the judgments in which the absolute affirmation will be verified, in any order whatsoever, can be applied to it or count for it. In all judgments it is not so much that which is worth more than the judgments as that which is reflected in each of them. In all actions this affirmation is not so much that which transcends all of them as that from which all actions take their value. In this way it is not subject to judgment, for there is judgment only through it but no judgment of it. We cannot affirm absolute affirmation to be such and such unless it is already entirely in our judgment and is rejecting it. We cannot take it as the object of our judgment unless it is already the condition of that judgment and is contradicting it.

It also seems that pure consciousness of self, at the level of primary certitude, requires nothing more than the pure difference which is recreated unceasingly between the position of affirmation and the consciousness of the affirmation as such. Here, then, there is certainly a negation of the world, a forgetting of the concrete self, that is, of the real differences which cling to pure difference. These real differences require that hard work follow upon possession of my being, which the primary certitude gives me. They require subsequently an effort for possession of self in which are involved the givens from which consciousness abstracts in reflection. The absolute affirmation changes into a "let it be." Henceforth, however, an intensive infinite, evidence of the efficacy of the primary affirmation at every stage in the realization of a purpose or of an encounter of minds, is now joined to the unending effort which is pursued on levels where ever more subtle differences will keep appearing.

Far from marking with an illusory character historical and concrete action within the world and among minds, this absolute affirmation makes this action the dynamic encounter between pure consciousness of self and the world through the concrete self. For the self, to be is to effect this liaison and to acquire possession of self, in its partial success or in its failure. There is no longer anything in nature which can be indifferent, once consciousness knows that in nature and through it is effected the impossible verification of a certitude which has abstracted from all empirical being only to rediscover it with an increased devotion which transfigures it.

Nothing would be more false now than to oppose pure consciousness of self to concrete and real consciousness. To do so would be to pretend that the being of concrete consciousness or the being of the self pre-existed the genesis of possibilities and actions which together symbolize, express, and betray what, at the summit of reflection, is defined as pure position of self. Every ethic is doomed to impotency which does not require that the real powers of the human soul correspond to conditions by which it is defined in reflection. In a psychological perspective, the relationship of an interior act to the knowledge which it has of itself in motives and in imagination, in which it unfolds its first movements, corresponds to the relationship of pure consciousness of self to the concrete self. When we have become reflectively conscious of the being which we are through pure consciousness of self, it is true that we can accomplish no action in which the conditions to which the intimate act of consciousness is indebted for its realization and self-knowledge would not be implied. On the other hand, however, these manifest the inadequation between concrete existence and what one might call the exchange of the pure self with itself. It is for the same reason that the self must forgo the hope of ever being equal to itself and still always strive for this.

On the other hand, this is why it is impossible to designate as subjectivity the interiority to itself of pure consciousness of self in which rest is not distinguished from activity. For subjectivity to be born, some resistance must gather itself together, as out of nothing, making an operation aware of itself which at first made no difference within the self. The impossibility of self-adequation enters into the constitution of subjectivity. The self verifies at the height of its effort that it has not so much dominated its law of genesis as it has depended on it to deepen itself and create itself. In the barely discernible difference which always slips in between what it is and what it ought to be it discovers what makes it such, what makes it subjectivity, and what explains that neither failure, nor fault, nor solitude can be spared it. This movement from pure consciousness of self to subjectivity is then movement to real consciousness. While expansion and a going-out from the self make consciousness risk alienation of its being, they also make possible a concrete experience of the self in interpersonal relations and in action. If in some minds this effort exalts itself into an immediate sacrificial willingness, is it any-thing more than a sign of a rash but irreproachable desire to span the distance which keeps opening up between the being which they become in action and the being which they are in the interiority of reflection? Pure consciousness of self which would be, at the same time, a complete real consciousness would have no need of the world or of historical action in order to possess itself progressively in unending risk.

As long as consciousness keeps trying to understand itself in terms of its past, its faults, and failure, there is something like a tension between the interest of the self in itself and the anticipa-tion of some certitude capable of saving it. When this tension changes over into an affirmation which frees the self, it also gives way to an experience in which the relationship of real consciousness to pure consciousness of self is emotionally trans-lated. This experience accompanies the exercise of our activities the way a deep, indeterminate feeling lends to all states of the soul, particularized in their object, a quality which of themselves they would not have possessed. However, alternatively, this ex-perience also isolates itself. It is necessary that sometimes it isolate itself in order to restore all its meaning to the primary certitude. It includes the assurance that neither our past nor our faults can deprive us of the force of renewal and that at every moment a radical regrasping of our being, which is regeneration, is possible. So vital, so intense can our feelings then become that they seem no longer to owe their existence solely to the relation-ship which they have to the primary certitude. This is why these feelings often claim another source, as though they were of the same kind as those aroused in our soul by a dialogue with beings whom we invoke and who respond. It may be a feeling of invulnerability, the experience of a life no longer centered on self, which marks with a kind of unreality many givens to which consciousness believed itself bound. It may be the greater depth of our attachment to beings, allied to an undefinable renunciation of all interest which concerns our own self. It may be an increase in our attention to the density of historical time, correlative to the certitude that it is still only the necessary figure of acts which emerge from it. It may be a feeling of confidence, intensified by a kind of indifference to success. It may be the feeling of regeneration, which does not so much wipe out our past as it sorts it out, simplifies it, and gives us the assurance of recourse.

Neither devotion nor asceticism nor actions which are at the summit of morality and appear sometimes to belong to still another order than the moral are in question here. If there are individual actions which, in the immanent order, are such that we have the right or the duty to consider them as expressions of pure consciousness of self and as exempt from all attachment to nature, this is not a question to be posed while we are on the level of this experience, which concerns only the interior acts of consciousness. Such acts do not tend to change the face of the world. There is no question of establishing a hierarchy among them. They involve a suspension of intentions seeking ends. Consciousness gathers itself in, loosens the ties which bind it to the world, refuses to confuse its being with the self which is made by its history, and attains, behind the self involved in effort or in friendship, a self which is for itself only the concrete and singular mode of an affirmation which affirms itself in this self, which is this self but also surpasses this self absolutely. This affirmation is such that it does not cease to offer itself in its affirmability to a consciousness aspiring to take charge of itself. From this it follows that, when it returns to self, consciousness does not attribute to itself the causality of this return any more than it has momentarily to answer for itself, to confront, to say "I." The affirmation affirmed in it saves it from the anxiety of causality; this anxiety is only postponed—this it knows. However, along with the anxiety of causality are also erased the emotions which normally accompany it. For these emotions, for the self-love they touch on, for the self-interests they echo, there is substituted a feeling which is not so much contentment or joy as rediscovered security in the detachment which comes with regard to the future of one's own self. The self neither asks nor obtains redemption or pardon for its past, nor does it set about hiding it or blotting out the memory of it. But, momentarily, the past is impotent to affect consciousness, and in this impotency a transmutation readies itself. As long and as often as this experience is renewed, the self feels itself first of all discharged of the weight of its past. It no longer has to unravel the snarl of liberty and fatality presented to it in its actions.

Nevertheless, this experience, through the interior acts which constitute it, is not an enclave in the becoming of the self, after which nothing in it will be changed. Nor is it the summit of a history, the consummation of a trial, which would make any suggestion of return to the temporal conditions of action appear to be a weakness. This experience inserts itself into the history of the self or interrupts it in order to transfigure the meaning of the self. Its present is not filled by the intuition of an essence in which eternity would remake all temporality into either a succession of degradations or an approach toward a liberation from time, doing so by means of stages emptied of all interest as soon as the illusory character of duration is discovered through them. It is not the prefiguration or the anticipation of a victory over temporality to which would aspire a consciousness living the experience of a trial or of a fall which has separated it from its source.

By shedding from its being all that would keep it from being only a mode through which pure consciousness of self affirms itself, the self withdraws from the world and from nature, just as this affirmation withdraws from history, in order to be entirely transparent to the operation which engenders it. Since this operation is never lacking to a consciousness which asks for it, it is true to say that it communicates its own character to the present which it occupies or which it touches. There is no history of the pure consciousness which regenerates me any more than there is a history of the discontinuous acts and instants in which this regeneration is realized. However, for a self bound to succession, this regeneration converts itself into a desire, into a willingness, to constitute a history which would be like the continuous phenomenon of those thin presents touched by the eternal.

Thus, also, the experience which we are here describing, far from tending to last and to sustain itself for its own sake, gives way to acts of realization. In this way feelings can cooperate and coexist in the same consciousness which would have been incompatible if the present in which consciousness got hold of itself in its source really detached it from the duration in which it unfolds and constructs itself. Thus it seems that consciousness can be freed from the world and yet lend it its forces, be indifferent to history and yet put off no action which concerns it, be ready for failure and neglect nothing which would favor the growth of morality. Consciousness cannot be duped by what one might expect from society and yet work for the transformation of human relations, cannot misunderstand what an idea is, in the purity of its act, and yet act as if certain ideas should triumph over nature. The relationship of duration to this pure present becomes the relationship of concrete acts of an active consciousness to interior acts of a subjectivity in which pure consciousness of self is affirmed. Instead of inciting us to depreciate the causes to which we are devoted, this experience immunizes us against despair, which can be born, on the historical level, of the limitations imposed on creation by the degradation of ideas, by all that is uncertain and unachieved in the most accomplished destinies. These two rhythms, which are contrary, if one isolates them, require each other and complement each other in a consciousness simultaneously attentive to the intimateness of its principle and to the expansion of its effort.

This alliance of feelings which abstraction isolates is the expression of the solidarity of temporal forms, that is, of relationships which the dimensions of time set up in a consciousness capable of different functions. Without prejudice one can approach these affective structures from temporal relationships or disengage these temporal relationships from the deepening of affective experiences. Undoubtedly, there is no active or passive feeling of the soul which is not linked to a relationship in which the dimensions of time receive, respectively, a particular value from the function exercised by consciousness. At the beginning of reflection on fault and solitude we saw the past usurp the first place, occupy the present, and block the future. The diversity of feelings, which are at the origin of the movement of reflection, is evidence of the prevalence of a past which is such that the present, even though it flows along, no longer seems to be able to assume a future. However, the recollection of consciousness, based on primary certitude, makes it possible for the life of the self, in the practice of morality, to trust in hope and restore to the future its full worth. It can do so without failing to have at each moment the experience of a feeling which binds it to the highest affirmation and maintains its actuality within a present directed toward the promotion of values. Without getting confused, without struggling with one another, the invariance of primary certitude and the choice of a certain tension within temporality concert in the present as do the feelings of the soul, its hope, and its security. The feeling of a possession which has nothing to fear from time is joined to the pursuit of goals.

5 / Promotion of Values

THE MOVEMENT OF REFLECTION does not direct itself toward primary affirmation so that it may settle down in it. It does this so that the existence of the self, as it produces itself out of desire at all levels of action, will imitate and verify as much as possible this primary certitude. Experiences analogous to those of fault and solitude will always assert themselves to some degree at all levels. However, the inadequation of existence to itself gradually changes meaning as the self acquires a more lucid awareness of the conditions in which disappointment must necessarily be mixed with satisfaction. The primacy of pure consciousness of self excludes the idea of progress, of an unfolding of existence which would respond to its principle. If moral philosophy refused to allow itself to be seduced by the prestige of speculative dialectics, which end in a kind of return of consciousness to its principle and to the fullness of being, it would recognize that the highest success of existence is not exempt from the menace of corruption. Nothing prevails against the fact that, at the level of history, action and effort block any hope of victory over the conditions which require them. For this reason, we have alternation between concentration of the self at its source and its expansion in the world.

This alternation, as well as this alliance, of reflection, which returns to its principle, and of the promotion of existence in action is found at all levels of an ethic. As long as the self has not found the way to read itself in the text which it traces in its own acts, it cannot understand the relationship which is unceasingly realized between pure consciousness of self and real exist-

[57]

ence. It is this fundamental relationship which is rediscovered at the foundation of the idea of value. What reflection grasps and affirms as pure consciousness of self the self appropriates as value to the extent that it creates itself and becomes really for itself. This means that value appears in view of existence and for existence when pure consciousness of self has turned toward the world to become the principle or rule of action and, at the same time, the measure of satisfaction in a concrete consciousness. Value is always linked to a certain obfuscation of the principle on which it is based and which sustains it. Value would not be value if it did not have in it something which makes us think that it does not exhaust the principle which it symbolizes or verifies. All efforts and actions which are evidence of value make us experience the inadequation which remains between the fullest and richest action and the interior act from which it proceeds. This obfuscation of the generative principle of value stimulates the desire to promote value within the resistance born of the very success of our effort. However, it has nothing in common with a kind of spiritual degradation of a principle which would contain, in an eminent manner, all the value that our efforts and actions manifest. This obfuscation of the generative principle of value signifies that this principle cannot be grasped under the sign of value unless it is involved in an effort or action which does not aim directly at the realization or actualization of its principle but is an effort willed first of all for its intrinsic signification. Promotion of value can only be indirect. In this respect, the obfuscation of the generative principle of value is the expression of a law which affects all manifestations of the human spirit. What Maine de Biran says about signs, that is, about acts which reveal its constitutive power to consciousness, must also be said about values. The act which becomes a sign gets involved in an operation and loses, "in order to illuminate itself, that portion of light" which it communicates to the material elements in which it is involved.[1] Likewise, every creative act can promote value, and esteem and know itself, only if it agrees to involve itself in an effort, in an action where at first we lose track of it. This is not an abatement or weakening of the principle. For this reason, we can already understand the opposition between a philosophy of intelligibility and a philosophy of

1. Cf. Pierre Maine de Biran, *Mémoire sur la décomposition de la pensée* (Paris: Editions Tisserand, 1920–42), IV, 235.

value. A philosophy of intelligibility avoids the material, since contact with it seems to it to be an indication of a passivity or a weakness of human consciousness. A philosophy of value converts the material into sign and makes of this conversion the operation which constitutes value itself. However, it also seems that this operation runs the risk of betraying the generative principle of value. It is the indispensable test without which no consciousness can enter into possession of itself and of its law.

From this point of view, one can already judge that the principle at the root of the values of existence and action cannot itself be a value. Consciousness does not share in this principle as if there were a superabundance of being in the principle which would also be a superabundance of value. In its acquisition as well as in its possession, every value remains inseparable from an interior movement of existence to produce or maintain itself. Every value remains subject to possible loss, forgetfulness, or degeneration. If we succumb to the temptation of conceiving the principle of values in imitation of, or according to, the model of values which are evidence of an advance or promotion of existence in the world, we do nothing else but reproduce and locate them outside the beings in which they appear. We forge universals for them which precede and sustain them. The relationship of a singular judgment of truth to truth is not that of partial knowledge to integral knowledge, which would exist before partial knowledge and contain it. It is rather the relationship of an operation, always in some way historical, to the unconditionality of the intention which is immanent in the operation. It is an intention which other operations must always realize. Likewise, the relationship of a particular value, which breaks forth in action or manifests itself in a being, to value is not that of partial manifestation and partial expression to the totality of value. It is rather the relationship of a promotion of existence to an absolute intention which no success can exhaust or satisfy. Each of these successes is a kind of transaction between this pure creative intention and the conditions in which the promotion of existence or of morality is realized. The idea of value has to arise when belief in an active superreality or in an intelligible world weakens. This superreality or this intelligible world purports to be the spiritual locus of all that we obtain or create, on the contrary, only in an indirect manner through the relationship of a generative intention to action and to the world.

Whether we are witnesses or actors, no value can be disassociated from the emotion which we experience in the presence of beings, actions, or efforts serving an intention which is not of this world even though it must be involved in the world to promote existence. The predicate, the quality, which value is, instead of participating in an essence, translates an act, an intention, which could not even interiorly be assured of itself without a modicum of action, without the mediation of history and of enterprises.

If there is a difference between what we are accustomed to call judgments of value and judgments of reality, it is to be found in the nature of the predicate. In judgments of reality, the predicate, in categorical judgments, belongs to a genus, by which the subject of the judgment is specified. In hypothetical judgments, the predicate expresses a quality linked by right to another quality, as soon as the former quality is present in a given subject. In judgments of value, the being of the subject, action, effort, or person serves a quality which is a reflection on it of an act, or a creative operation, of a pure intention at the very moment when this act, bending toward the world to produce and grasp itself indirectly in the world, becomes a source of value because of the resistance which it encounters or occasions. Consequently, in the predicate of a judgment of value is hidden an unconditional position which no reality can equal. Nevertheless, this reality, or the creative process which constitutes it, allows the act of this positioning to attain to possession of itself by means of value instead of indefinitely returning to itself in unconsciousness of self. Thus, the act of pure consciousness of self is beyond value. Value arises when pure affirmation, becoming idea, infinite exigency, turned henceforth toward the world and toward life, exposes itself to resistance concomitant with creative becoming, in order to assure itself of itself. At the basis of every value there is something like a pretension of obtaining from the real and from life an expression of what transcends all expression and all realization. It would do this either by creating or by utilizing the real. The intention manifested in the predicate is not itself a judgment even though it rules the judgment or gives foundation to it, since it is superior to all attribution and to all determination. Instead of being a partial determination of reality, a point of view on the totality of qualities or properties of a given subject, instead of being able to be completed by other determinations, the predicate of a judgment of value transmits to a subject, a being, or an action a quality which cannot be considered analytically in a totality and in the comprehension of a given reality. The subject receives the predicate of value by a sort of borrowing or gratuity. The generative act of the predicate, insofar as it transcends singular predications, is a ferment of dissatisfaction in each of them. The formula *omnis determinatio est negatio* radically changes meaning for values. In this instance this formula does not designate the incompleteness of a judgment due to the splitting-up of the real any more than it is evidence of the partiality of our perspective on the whole of being or of its reflection in an individual consciousness. On the contrary, this formula suggests that we consider that an action, an effort, affected by a predicate of value, claims to be nothing more than a means, an instrument, by which creative affirmation succeeds in giving evidence of itself in the world.

Failing to understand the meaning of the predicate in the judgment of value, consciousness misunderstands the relationship of value to the world as well as the relationship of value to pure intention and to the act from which it proceeds. The world refuses value, lends itself to it, disappoints hope and satisfies it. Impatience with regard to an impossible adequation between acts, the creative intentions which give foundations to the predicates of value or qualities *and* the subjects or beings which serve them, incites consciousness both to deny that the world is capable of value and to abandon itself to quasi-desperate actions to realize, all at once, all value in reality. What is most difficult to maintain at the center of consciousness is the idea that danger, risk, and difficulty are always as great, that at best they change exteriorly, and at the same time to maintain the certitude that their growth does not block the reconciliation of willing with itself. In a judgment of value, the predicate is the expression of an appeal which an act of pure consciousness of self, which transcends all reality, addresses to reality. However, this act takes on as many ideas and pure intentions as there are functions of concrete consciousness in the infinite diversity of historical conditions in which this consciousness acts within the world. A philosophical ethic can serve the highest interests of consciousness by showing that dangers can become more subtle and resistance less visible but not less strong. It can also serve these interests by instigating a kind of promotion of these difficulties in spheres more and more distant from the primitive forms of combat. Finally, it can also serve by teaching concrete consciousness that there is no defeat which cannot be victory and no victory which cannot be undone and that there is no return to the interiority of pure consciousness by means of value.

If the source of the predicate in a value judgment is an idea, a creative intention, which is itself an expression of pure consciousness of self when this latter becomes exigency of action and realization in a concrete consciousness, one must also be able to account for a negative predicate which expresses not only the absence of a desired value but the presence of an opposite quality. The form of the judgment should not mislead us. We not only deny that an action is courageous; we affirm that it is cowardly. Here in the judgment there are two distinct but united moments. The act of negation refers to an idea which would authorize us to hope for and even to demand the presence of a positive value in an effort and in action. This act of negation is completed by the admission that, in fact, a predicate which is not only other, but also contrary, must be attributed to the action or the effort. Would this be possible if the supra-oppositional principle were already in itself value? One can well conceive that a value might present itself in different degrees and, from this point of view, seem to degenerate but not that it would turn against itself, so to speak. The obfuscation of the generative principle of value is one thing; the opposition of a value and a countervalue is another thing. The first translates the impossibility for the principle, for pure consciousness, for creative intention in whatever order it determines itself, to bear witness to itself in anything but an indirect manner in a finality whose significance is intrinsic to the world. The second is the generation of its opposite at the level of the operation which should give birth to value; it is not merely an impotent or awkward effort. Nothing is more real than actions affected by negative-sign quality. These actions are in no way comparable to negations which suspend doubtful affirmations. They are efficacious, and by their influence on the total intellectual and moral organism these negative actions do not so much delay or slow down the ascending movement of consciousness as they bring it back, abruptly, well below the point which the promotion of values had attained.

When we do not distinguish values from their principle, which, properly speaking, is not a value, we are constrained to have recourse to a kind of degeneration or inversion of the highest value in order to account for qualities which are negations of values. However, there can be no contrary of this value, which is always shared in or active in some way. Opposition is nothing more than an illusion of contrariety produced by simultaneous consideration of values very distant from one another because of their degree of participation. Consequently, they are values which are very unequal in richness and force. Negation ceases to be serious. It arranges degrees or steps so that acquisition of value will not be too rapid. But value is never really menaced. The grain of liberty involved beforehand in value is only destined to maintain some distance between being in its fullness and the movement of a particular consciousness. Insofar as a history is conceivable, negation delays its progress, giving way, however, as soon as it has carried out its function.

It is otherwise if the supra-oppositional principle is not itself value. The generative act of value activates subjectivity, i.e., liberty, which is not to be confused with pure consciousness. No pure intention, no idea, can be generative of value without involving the consent and adherence of subjectivity. A generative idea of value is efficacious only because of the complicity of a liberty which is never out of the picture, even when concrete consciousness fails to distinguish itself from the intention which animates it or from the idea which inspires it. This is the case no matter how intimate the relationship of a generative idea is, on the one hand, to pure consciousness and, on the other hand, to efforts or actions in which this generative idea might appear to be value. Liberty has this irreplaceable role in value, but it also has this responsibility in actions affected by a predicate opposed to the predicate of value.

We notice, first of all, that pairs of qualities, courageous and cowardly, pure and impure, generous and avaricious, do not designate contraries which could be considered as extremes in a single genus which would include each member of a pair. Their opposition stands out against the background of an irremediable contradiction, and this contradiction itself is the expression of the fact that real consciousness includes a twofold relationship. It is related both to pure consciousness, which affirms itself in it, and to that which cannot enter into the same genus as pure consciousness, to that which is in absolute opposition to it. There would be no opposition between predicates of value if there were not a supra-oppositional principle and an infra-oppositional principle of value. The region of concrete consciousness is where intentions and motives meet, share in one another, and become contraries through the complicity of liberty. This they do before being translated into actions through qualities which judgment will designate as opposed predicates forming a pair.

However, in speaking of an infra-oppositional principle of value, or, more exactly, of its contrary—for it is very evident that the idea of a negative value is, literally, nonsense—we avoid trying to realize it as such. It is nothing that one can get hold of, because it always assumes the form of each of our faults, weaknesses, or failures as well as the form of each delay in the advance of nature toward beauty. Nevertheless, the two opposed directions in which action takes place—action which engenders value or its contrary—are determined by this infra-oppositional principle. The language which fixes value in the predicate makes us forget that beneath the quality there is the rhythm of action which expresses itself in it. There is something like a shiver which erases the seeming immobility of our life. Not to be worthwhile or not to wish to be worthwhile is an action as certain as to be worthwhile. It is a weakening, an abatement, of interior energy accompanied by the consent and secret complacency of consciousness. Concrete reality adds up, but more often neutralizes reciprocally, successes and betrayals. If we wanted to form a myetaphysical idea of concrete reality, it would be necessary to conceive it according to the model of this becoming which we experience in the depths of ourselves. One cannot say that concrete reality is produced by a continuous advance in a single direction. Opposed processes battle one another, are astride one another, in concrete reality; equilibriums are realized and undone, and no form is concretely created which is not immediately menaced interiorly. In concrete reality, value and its contrary are indefatigable rivals, and, no more than shadow is made only from lack of light, can one pass by imperceptible stages of debasement from value to its contrary.

When it is a question of value judgments, negation manifests this opposition clearly. Through the subject, to which judgment refuses to assign this or that quality, the predicate leads back to an operation, an intention, which is its foundation. It is not an essence in which the subject participates and which defines it. This is why negation is not simple privation, which, excluding the subject from participation in this or that essence, would leave undetermined the quality which belongs to it. If the negation expresses itself in terms of value in refusing it to the subject, it is in order to make the point that this value is not only the one we expected it to have but the one it should have and which by rights one should demand of it. Beneath the negation in a value judgment one can discern, in the expressions in which consciousness translates its regret, blame, and reprobation, the various modes according to which a given quality of truth, loyalty, or beauty is susceptible of being required of a given action, behavior, or affirmation in every order of value and within this order. However, the absence of this quality is the presence of a contrary quality. Negation does not leave open the question of knowing what quality the subject possesses. Negation can immediately change into an affirmation whose quality is opposed to that which the subject should have possessed. We know what predicate belongs to a given action which under the circumstances ought to have been courageous. Thus, negation relies on the idea of an "ought" which consciousness denies has been understood so as not to directly affirm that it has been betrayed. However, inversely, negation, instead of being blame or regret, is protestation against an accusation or a doubt when the predicate in a negative judgment relates to the quality contrary to the value which the subject must or ought to have possessed. At the same time, negation is affirmation of the value which was denied the subject. It restores the correct relationship between action and the value judgment. I cannot say that a man is a liar without affirming that he is, as he ought to be, capable of truth. Certainly, subsequently, nothing obliges one to say that there cannot be or that there are not degrees of value or of its contrary. But there is no position of indifference. Negation in a value judgment attests that not only is the idea of "ought" in all its generality present at the foundation of the idea of value but that neither of the two contrary directions to which the predicate relates can be deprived of the other. We can conclude from this that there is opposition between value and its contrary only against the background of an absolute contradiction, a contradiction which is not only dialectic or relative, a contradiction between the nonbeing which is basic to this opposition and that which is beyond it and beyond value. The destiny of consciousness is played out entirely in the *entre-deux.*

It follows that a predicate of value which we express in a judgment, and which seems to us to belong to an action or a being, leads us back to a principle which no judgment can enclose. If we wish to judge this principle, we must acknowledge that the judgment we make has its source entirely in the law which generates a predicate which can be found in a multiplicity of singular judgments but which assigns this predicate to no definite subject. In consciousness, an act, a fundamental intention which expresses the interior rhythm of its existence, corresponds to this generative law.

Because of this, one can appreciate what is seductive and specious in an ethic which relies on values considered as essences offering themselves to intuition before being realized or effected in conduct. Predicates of value seem to subordinate themselves to intentions, to directions of intention which they only seem to illustrate. Will one make essences of these intentional directions? One resigns oneself to begin an examination of acts constitutive of an ethic prior to the moment where such essences are constituted. Forgetting that it is characteristic of the human spirit to be affected by its own creations, one misunderstands the nature of these acts. Living an autonomous life because of the interior necessity placed in them by the act from which they proceed, creations of the human spirit detach themselves from the human spirit and subsequently impose themselves on an individual consciousness. Consciousness no longer has so much to reinvent as to maintain the authority of, and unceasingly to appropriate, those creations. The creations, the rhythms of intimate existence, from which the creative act seems to have withdrawn to offer itself for imitation or verification, are what consciousness believes it contemplates outside itself or what it believes it grasps in intuition. There is no essence which is not one of these rhythms. Imagination, which takes possession of them, no longer has to produce them but accepts control of them. Since most often we take neither the time nor the trouble to develop this schema, to prolong the movement which is sketched in us, we become more sensitive to the independence which this schema possesses with respect to the discontinuous and changing life of consciousness. But how would this intimate necessity guide consciousness in its judgments, in its evaluations, how could it regulate the play of its emotions, if it did not itself have its source in a productivity where there is not yet any duality between the generative movement and the interior law of this movement?

Since it is necessary to bring these essences closer to the subject of action to make them the source of duty, since it is necessary to recognize that the modal categories of theoretical thought—and, in particular, the relationship of the possible to the necessary and to the real—are not valid for these value-essences, which have rather to create the conditions making possible their realization, the defenders of this position admit the fundamental difference between the "free necessity" of essence and the necessity of the real. Immanent in these essences there is an inclination to realization and an ideal "oughtness." Consequently, there is in the essence itself a relationship to eventual operations and actions of the subject. This relationship is sufficient evidence that, even if the necessity of these essences transcends an individual consciousness as such, it is not at all independent of the operations of pure consciousness undertaking the creation of an ethical order. It is patent that the ideality of value-essences is nothing more than the ideality of creations, of permanent directions born of productive imagination which have become rules for action and evaluation for the individual consciousness. They are clothed, certainly, in an authority which transcends the contingent movements of an individual consciousness. However, only the twofold character of the human spirit, capable at once of creating and of affecting itself by its own creations, gives a specious character to the transcendence of essences.

We can maintain, then, for values, the difference between a formal a priori and a material a priori as long as it is reduced to the difference between an a priori expressing in the most exact manner the relationship of pure consciousness to concrete consciousness and an a priori where this first relationship, determining itself as a function of certain characteristics or inclinations of the subject of action, communicates its authority to the already specialized pure intentions of an active consciousness. Thus a material a priori would open out on an open multiplicity of acts whose internal similarity would be translated by an identical predicate of value. What founds the identity of the predicate is always a certain rhythm which directs the most intimate movements of the acting being to itself and regulates them. We attempt to rediscover this rhythm in values which seem to express a *habitus* of the subject more than a relationship of pure consciousness to the concrete self, which always seems to imply to some degree both duty and an appeal to liberty. This is the case with gentleness, with purity, and with all the other qualities exempt from tension and effort which, less successfully than all others, the subject would vainly attempt to effect directly in his actions and to appropriate by his decision. The more that he will have desired and sought those qualities as such, the less will they shine forth in him. Nevertheless, here again, we believe that we perceive within these qualities, and beneath the predicates by which we designate them, the presence and the efficacy of diverse rhythms to which all movements of the soul and the trembling of the interior life are spontaneously docile. We would not hesitate to recognize beneath all these values the rhythms which command them if we were not accustomed to designating by the single name value both the qualities which shine forth in actions and efforts and these dynamic forms, these rhythms, which are their true foundation and which are linked in each consciousness to its most profound experience of being. By constituting the values as essences, one concentrates in them the predicate, instead of seeking to surprise the passage of pure action of consciousness to the quality by which it becomes accessible.

Without this distinction between the process interior to creative consciousness and the quality, the predicate of value, a distinction toward which all the preceding analyses have tended, one would get involved in difficulties which weigh down on the entire development of an ethic. It is not at all assured that this process, this generative act, experiences itself as a function of qualities in which it is in a way objectified and which the predicate expresses. To be worthwhile for a consciousness is to be this process, but it is not to see itself through the medium of the qualities which appear in its accomplished action and whose judge it hardly is. A consciousness *is* to the extent that it does not aim at the predicates by which we designate values. Consciousness wills the operations which engender these values, but it wills them for themselves and not for the qualities which will aid it to esteem or to disdain the accomplished action. Value would go against the effort to be worthwhile, which is the foundation of value, if the effort to be worthwhile regulated itself according to value.

As long as the generative act of value is where it should be—in sensibility, where it manifests itself—it produces a transfiguration there. When it withdraws from sensibility, the actuality of the value comes to an end. Just as a look is veiled when the soul refuses love, so nature is suddenly deprived of meaning and words are emptied of their substance. Nevertheless, the memory of experiences of value remains, not only as a form of nostalgia, but as a direction for thought or for willing which other experiences will actualize. If we conceive the relationship of the a priori which is at the source of value to value itself, sensibility no longer has to be reduced to intelligible elements. Value protects and rehabilitates sensibility, without which consciousness would not be able to take its own measure. Besides, when the opposition between the intelligible and the sensible overlaps, or is confused with, the opposition between pure thought and individual sensibility, it could not be otherwise than that feeling would be discarded as pathological, to speak as Kant does, or be taken for the confused expression of intellectual relationships. The question changes meaning when it appears that the generative a priori of value is a process which unfolds itself in symbols, where it attains self-assurance. Feeling is the omnipresence of this operation to the soul where it is produced and whose movements it regulates. It has meaning because of the interior regulation which it accepts and which ennobles it. It follows that growing satisfaction in the presence of a value is not to be confused with pleasure properly speaking. Because it is fused with the generative law of value, a consciousness enjoying satisfaction is not subject to a nature, to inclinations, removed from the action of liberty. When pleasure has already ceased, satisfaction remains and maintains itself by an interior movement which animates it. The effort of an active or creative consciousness is accompanied by renunciation in favor of value and by submission to an internal necessity which must harmonize with the order of the world. However, subsequently, consciousness cannot deepen the satisfaction which it experiences without soon discovering that it is itself freely affected and receives the benefit of its renunciation. The exercise of the faculties of consciousness which engenders satisfaction echoes the generative activity of value. Consciousness welcomes itself, even though it cannot avoid linking its satisfaction to a realized value. Henceforth, satisfaction derives its quality from its participation in an order which transcends that of natural inclination. Postponed, subordinated to a discipline required for the generation of value, satisfaction becomes capable of renewal, of a deepening which is no longer subject to the laws of satiety or of exhaustion. Rays, coming from another focal point, penetrate and illumine sensuality.

We can no longer postpone an examination of the relationship of action and existential values, which we have just studied, to other groups of values. It is a decisive problem for any ethic, but particularly for an ethic which proceeds from consciousness. However, no doctrine can escape the twofold obligation of respecting or of saving the intrinsic meaning of different groups of values and of having them communicate, or even of establishing their hierarchy. One would think that the best doctrines for giving a foundation to this communication of values and their affinities would be those which do not separate value from being or from a superreality and which think that being is implicated in every value, although differently and unequally. The varieties of metaphysical idealism are here in agreement, and they are also in agreement with the most decided metaphysical realism. They agree not only to leave values discontinuous and without link but to root them in being, in being that is thought, or in the concrete universal, or in a *natura naturans* understood in any way as long as it is a generative power of which all values would be the expression or particularization.

However, how could one reconcile the ontological unity of reality and the unity of value one expects to be linked to it with the apparent plurality of values? The ultimate value is in the whole, and value rises with participation in it.[2] This is, undoubtedly, the theme which one finds in doctrines of very diverse inspiration, whether they climb toward an absolute experience, where they concentrate all values or in which all values are absorbed with their own characteristics effaced, or whether they proceed from the unity of being in order to derive the multiplicity of values. To each increase of participation in the whole

2. Bernard Bosanquet. *The Principle of Individuality and Value* (London: Macmillan, 1912), p. 342: "The ultimate value is in the whole, and value rises with participation in it. . . ."

corresponds a transfiguration of the experience of value which dims the brilliance of value of an inferior degree. To each withdrawal with regard to the highest reality, or the superreality, corresponds a diminution of being which is also a diminution and change of value.

All the same, if at the start one does not begin to project into reality or into the *natura naturans,* in an eminent form, each of the values for which foundations must be found, how can an unequal participation in the same principle translate itself for consciousness by the experience of values qualitatively irreducible? Is a contingent intervention of consciousness at the root of the plurality and the differentiation of values? Is this intervention of consciousness the sign of some unknown partiality, the indication of its impotency and its finitude, or the expression of a function which it exercises and which it assumes? It is necessary that there be some proportion, some affinity, between consciousness and the being which it grasps. But the idea of multiple functions of consciousness, in this perspective, does not so much witness to a plural operative character as to a plural relationship to certain aspects of total reality. These are so many spiritual abstractions. The contingent energy by which a subject, with its desires or with its own will, isolates in being what it retains as value, is itself the expression of the place which this subject occupies in the hierarchy of beings and of being. Value is differentiated to the extent that being is refracted by a diversity of minds or of beings placed perhaps at different moments of the evolution of reality itself. Progress in knowledge and in the experience of value of a subject can only be made by an expansion, an enlargement, of its vision, which is a renunciation of all isolation. Each of these abstractions is a betrayal with regard to the whole and a misunderstanding of the participation of beings in being and of values in value. Thus the values of action, the values of an ethic properly speaking, are linked to the effort incumbent on the individual consciousness to place itself in its own truth, that is, in the truth of the whole. Subordinated in both their orientation and their foundation to the reality of the concrete universal, these values are evidence of the imperfection inherent in a consciousness which draws on a premonition of total being for the force which it uses to break the illusion of separation and of isolation of beings in being. At the end of this effort, how could beauty, truth, and morality not be merged in a single vision, in a unique experience of value, in a single pleasure in rediscovered being? To reserve some autonomy for different values, the metaphysical experience of total being must be deferred; it must draw back, inaccessible, the closer consciousness believes that it approaches it. Then it would be true, undoubtedly, that, diffused in limited and incomplete experiences, reality would communicate to each of them some value. But how will one determine, as a function of an absolute experience of which we have only an idea, the proportion of being which enters into each value and which assigns its level to it? Why in consciousness is this difference of degree equal to the experience of heterogeneous values? If absolute experience escapes us, if we lack an experience which would allow us to unite ourselves to being and be present at a kind of breaking-up or differentiation of value in turning our attention to its unity, then the idea of the concrete universal remains only a method, an invitation addressed to consciousness so that it will not leave values unordered and without hierarchy. Under the protection of this agnosticism, values unfold the richness of their content. The pole where their differences would be effaced remains unattainable. Insensibly, one returns to relating these differences to functions of the human spirit, asking the subject to master their plurality so as not to make impossible the intercourse of values in a single consciousness. But then it is no longer a consubstantial unity of all values which is shared in them and which unfolds unequally in them. From the unity of being and of value one returns to an immanent analysis illuminating its own progress, an analysis of pure generative intentions of different orders of values.

If the conditions under which the life of man is lived, no less than his own inclinations, lend themselves in fact to a plurality of values, this completely potential plurality is not asserted, is not truly determined, except by the energy of consciousness and by the promotion which it effects in the exercise, in the signification, of spontaneous movements, emotions, actions, or reactions born in the presence of the world. These perceptions, these nascent actions, these emotions are the expression of man's commerce with the world. The lines which this commerce follows in its natural and spontaneous accomplishment in human experience design various possible groups of values. But what is necessary is a conversion of spontaneity into a pure intention and, through this latter, a promotion, a creation, of value in efforts and in acts.

One should not be surprised that it is very difficult to discover the spontaneous movements of the soul in efforts and in actions where value appears. This is so because these emotions, these movements, and the inclinations which carry them, far from producing these values by a simple expansion of their power, must, on the contrary, be controlled, mastered, or so profoundly transformed and carried to a different level that there is no longer any apparent trace in the values of the primitive conditions which were their cradle.

For example, in the value by which a work of art moves us, how do we discern the first movements of consciousness, which are more oriented to the direct possession of the object for the satisfaction of inclinations? If the commerce between sensibility and the world which these inclinations command sometimes manifests something like the beginning of a regrasping of consciousness through the instrumentality of the object, either because of the design or in some other way that manifests the properly aesthetic relationship, true value requires that within the inclination an action be produced which represses the spontaneous development and rules it by submitting it to a pure intention. One would seek in vain to bypass the moment when consciousness, so to speak, goes back over its emotions to throw new light on them, to liberate them from what was narrowly subjective in individual subjectivity, to make of them the matter of some work of art where they take on a secondary role in the service of an intention of communicable beauty. It is necessary to recognize that this creation of values plunges its roots into the spontaneous movements of affectivity and into the natural friendship between self and world. However, the relationship between the pure generative intention of an order of values and the first reactions of consciousness is hidden by the enrichment of sensibility. This enrichment is so decisive that it entails fear and protection with respect to the primitive givens of subjectivity. The strengthening of consciousness of value, the authority of efforts in which it finds support, conspire to make us forget this relationship. Between the first trait sketched by fingers eager to prolong the perception of a form and a work of art voluntarily produced with a view to renewable and communicable satisfaction, there is all the distance that separates desire from the premeditated accomplishment of a design. By inserting itself in desire, the pure intention of beauty unites it with the generative discipline of a work of art. It makes it share in a new power. However, this pure intention does not cease to nourish itself on the substance or to utilize the *élan* of desire.

If in all value and in every order of values there is to be an element of permanence opposed to whatever is capricious and changing in desire, value must include the equivalent of a rule, of a form, capable of directing desire and of imposing on it the unity of direction. However, desire itself welcomes or invokes these forms. They are born from models freely created by the will or by art and detach themselves from works of art and acts and, with respect to desire, become permanent directions for the satisfactions which desire anticipates or aims at. Desire lends itself to forms in which it discovers a sort of internal regulation by which it is removed from affective mobility. These forms are the work of our volitions, and we can grasp them only in these volitions. They are truly what make us will, prefer, appreciate otherwise than by the sole force of desire. But these forms are no longer anything if we abstract them from this will which they make will, from this sensibility which they make prefer, to give them a sufficiency in themselves and an existence for themselves. These forms are modes of a liberty which ties and links itself to itself to become active in a consciousness which wills or prefers. Liberty does so to lift consciousness above what it would have willed or preferred if it had only given in to the desire of nature.

Thus, in each province of the soul, the transfiguration of desire is realized by a pure intention. However, this pure intention cannot be separated from the operations, the efforts, the effective constructions where value appears. Because of these, an authority is constituted in every order which rules the exercise of satisfaction and subjects it to a discipline. When this discipline becomes an obstacle to the promotion of values, new forms put desire again under their power and guide it elsewhere. In effort we lose the trace of this liaison between pure intention and the forms in which it is involved. Nevertheless, it is through this liaison that pure intention imposes itself on desire and makes value appear. It is the task of reflection to rediscover in constructions, in regulated processes, in efforts, the pure intention which is the principle of value. But it is also the function of reflection to rediscover the spontaneous movements of the human soul which were the occasions out of which arose in every order an intention which transcends nature. Conditions of increased rigor, rules, forms, signs, languages, substitute perceptions and new actions for actions and perceptions rooted in instinct. The impoverishment of satisfaction which sometimes seems to result from this is compensated for by the possibility of renewing operations conducted according to rules. Each of the systems of symbols produced according to this effort of rigor is first of all a method of dissolution of the real as it is offered to immediate consciousness. By inventing these symbols, the human spirit discovers that it cannot give itself power over itself and over the world except by refusing to accept the world as such. This is why, at the source of every order of value, there is something like refusal of given reality, sustained by an *élan,* by an exaltation of consciousness which is communicated to imagination. So many values and symbolic forms enter into the movement of the real and of action that in our memory there is an obliteration of this nevertheless decisive moment when consciousness reacted most humbly against itself to assure itself of its creative power.

Each invention is more or less burdensome for man, especially since it asks him to be the faithful portrait of his most profound aspiration. What can help us understand in each case the meaning of a rupture with natural ends, the overturning, the backtracking of the spontaneous movements of nature, is what it costs man to substitute for primitive reality, for primitive perception, for primitive forms of action, a world and an order where the self obtains access to itself by the system of its own efforts. Man must get hold of himself and conquer himself with respect to what seemed to be readily offered to consciousness as the only commerce it could have with reality or with other minds. Man must first of all erase the characteristics of familiar reality and detect the promise of infinite conquest in the first attempts that follow upon this rupture, in the poverty, in the humility of his first successes, in the most humble design or in the most elementary verifications. What is burdensome in this operation is the renunciation of a vision of the real or of forms of action in accordance with inclinations. What is burdensome is the acceptance of an activity which at first seems to go against instinct. It is the initial consent to an ascesis of satisfaction, henceforth relative to the production of modes of expression or of action in which consciousness advances toward itself by changing unceasingly the sign of the real in which it was content. The genesis of an order of values, through a pure intention corresponding to it, is a problem of substitution where structures of reality become the support and matter of meanings at the permanent disposition of consciousness. Besides, by reaffirming its liberty with regard to these structures, consciousness gets hold of itself with respect to its own productions. These are productions accomplished in the unconsciousness of productive imagination and are so removed, subsequently, from its own power that they appear, in fact, as given nature. This will of consciousness to self-affirmation over sensible nature is nowhere, perhaps, better discerned than in the creation and promotion of values of beauty. Consciousness aspires to this self-affirmation only to serve the orchestration of nature recreated by the revelation of expressive forms for which nature had already provided some beginning. The very evident inferiority of the first attempts of art with respect to the successes of nature is evidence not only of a will to self-affirmation over the world but also evidence of a patience obstinate in discovery and in the creation of new means of expression susceptible of being substituted for those which were prepared by nature for the generation of values.

Motives, and concrete decision in which these motives take on flesh, unfold an interior act which becomes conscious only through them, even though these motives often seem to betray the interior act or to turn it in a direction where something coming from the world might be found to enter into composition. Likewise, pure intentions and the generative acts of value and, through them, the inexhaustible source from which all proceed, become perceptible to consciousness only through the first movements, the attempts where actions and efforts are sketched. Imagination effects the passage. However, it does not so much symbolize the invisible as it gives it the means to witness to its fecundity. It also gives consciousness the means with which to discern the quality of its intentions as well as the invincible reaction of the world, into which they penetrate, on these intentions themselves. Is it enough to say that these intentions penetrate there? Imagination is much more of a mediator between pure intention and a given world where value would only have to insert itself. It creates the instrument and the matter of value as much as the value itself. Imagination finds the residue of earlier acts already at its disposition in the world. Space and time show the trace of its unfolding. The duration which it tries to constitute or to inform by its own efforts keeps time, left behind it, from becoming inert. It keeps this time from serving exclusively a determinism which appears so very powerful only because one forgets the operations which preceded it.

Because of this twofold affirmation of pure intention over desire and over a given nature, value becomes the phenomenon, the attainable expression of an interior operation, which can assure itself as to what it is only by forcing itself toward this expression. Since this expression is invincibly subject to the laws of the phenomenon, on the one hand, it cannot help but be, in certain respects, an obfuscation of its generative principle and of the act, in its purity, or of the initiative which it makes visible. On the other hand, it is for this act the indispensable condition for measuring itself. That there is in this act a surplus which the expression does not exhaust and does not transmit into the phenomenon and value is verifiable only in and through the value, where the operation from which it proceeds and the sensible world in which it is enveloped interpenetrate. If the entire sensible world and all the beings with which we have dealings sometimes appear to us as a text to be deciphered, as the manifestation and appearance of an operation which was not able to find another expression, it is because the value in fact orders us to seek and discern the aspiration inscribed in our gropings, weaknesses, and failures of expression. At the level of the phenomenon, one never absolutely loses track of the operation which gives it a different meaning from the one it receives from the law and the linking of other phenomena in which it is grouped.

Nevertheless, the more the increase of efforts and the autonomy of the different orders of value and of the pure intentions from which they proceed are accentuated, the more the necessity grows for a determination of the relationship between the values of action and pure consciousness of self. If values do not vary as degrees of being vary or as moments of total reality are produced, it remains that the order instituted among values expresses the order which consciousness introduces into its essential intentions in view of its own possibilities of existence. One cannot think of reducing or of attenuating the distinction between generative intentions or orders of values without falling into the hypothesis which makes of them so many limited points of view, so many partial experiences susceptible of being corrected or completed to the extent that one achieves a higher or more concrete level. This is to return to the idea of a kind of disassociation of total reality by the partiality of the experiences of the subject. Then many values would have to appear in absolute experience, if not as illusory, at least as deprived of all proper consistency. Or it could happen that the prominence of one order of values over all others would entail for these others a kind of diminution. If, for example, beauty, sought for in metaphysically objective conditions, draws us as close as possible to absolute experience, because of the very affinity of its characteristics with total reality, it would shunt both mechanism and the truth of mechanism into the region of phenomena. If value is in universal being, is universal being, the hierarchy of values can only be the hierarchy of its expressions.

On the contrary, the idea of the unconditionality of the pure intention which gives foundation to an autonomous order of values is implied in the idea of such an order. It is true, on the one hand, that pure intentions agree formally in this, that all of them produce the awakening of consciousness to an order which is no longer the extension of desire. On the other hand, it is true that the autonomy of these intentions is not at all a synonym of competition. If the self cannot avoid being subject to the necessity of concentrating its forces and of giving itself unreservedly to the form of activity from which it expects the promotion of its own being, if it must then partially give up other values, there is nothing in this which touches on the intrinsic signification of the different orders. For the self, it is its being which is in question. Self-renunication has its source in the devotion of the self to chosen values. Consequently, it is not without compensation. Through this devotion consciousness remains closer to the generative act of values and more open to the inspiration which in every order renews or restores its freshness to the primary intention. The apparent narrowness of its choice is not at all an impoverishment for consciousness. From this point of view, no matter how diverse satisfactions are as to their sources, they complement one another to the extent that consciousness gives itself more to a single order of values which it deepens. The richness of satisfaction requires that values isolate themselves and separate from one another. This richness also requires each of the values to demand the exclusive attention of the self before the experience of reciprocal support, which they lend to one another, can be obtained, before we can experience the interpenetration of which values are capable.

Then, devotion to art or to science can coincide for the self with the expansion of its deep possibilities of existence. In all orders of values the self can work only indirectly in the interest of its own true being by aiming at actions or efforts or discoveries in their intrinsic signification. From this point of view, one avoids the depreciation of any order of values. It involves an ascesis which has its *raison d'être* in its own autonomy.

It is a question of knowing whether the values of truth and beauty lead us back reflectively to pure consciousness of self. These values, to which the self is devoted, would in this case be considered intrinsically and not with respect to promotion of the existence of the self, for which the self is indebted to these values. If such is the case, these intentions would not in themselves be unconditioned acts but would depend on the same certitude, the same affirmation, as the values of an ethic. All values would be equally illuminated by a single source of light. Here we rediscover another version of the postulate of an ontological theory of values according to which the highest reality eminently contains all value found in values for which it is the substantial link.

Nevertheless, there are good reasons for thinking that only values of action force reflecting consciousness to grasp, behind the pure intention which they prolong, the primary affirmation of pure consciousness of self. The autonomy, the more and more complete independence, of the order of truth and beauty with respect to religious consciousness, with which the ethical order is so strongly connected, is evidence of this fact. Whether they transfigure sensibility or enclose the world in their symbols, the values of truth or beauty include, along with their ambition of conquest and of renewal, the possibility of an intrinsic and direct deepening of their norms in relation to an always expected discovery which unceasingly changes the area to which reflection must address itself. This deepening is produced as a disassociation of self-consciousness, responsible for the destiny of the self, and intellectual or aesthetic consciousness. This happens in such a way that the subject, as it appropriates itself or creates the values of truth and beauty, tends more and more to enclose itself in the order which they constitute and to exclude jealously all intrusion of foreign exigencies. The irrealism of aesthetic values with respect to the concrete possibilities of the existence of the self makes of aesthetic satisfaction a kind of enclave in the flow of consciousness which is the correspondent of the whole which the work of art constitutes. Contemplation suspends momentarily all the other functions of the human spirit; for an instant it tears consciousness away from its own restlessness. In another sense, the true, by submitting consciousness to the rules of objectivity, induces it to consider all the other interests of the self as the expression of a subjectivity without authority and without value. At best, it is on the fringes of values obtained by devotion to these orders, which, properly, do not wish to recognize anything outside their own regulation, that a question is again formulated which leads the self back to itself and to its deep aspiration. It is the disappointment which these values occasion in the self with regard to the real accomplishment of its being that brings up this question.

There is no equivalent in the order of truth and of beauty of what in the order of values of action is constituted by the active negations represented by fault and evil. Neither error in pursuit of truth nor failure in the creation of beauty has any significance comparable to fault and failure, which interest the destiny of the self. It is not that the obfuscation of the generative principle of values is not felt. But the presence or the action of what is negative in experience is translated here only by privation of value.

Undoubtedly, resistance does not cease to arise. In spite of the help which nature offers the artist and which could sometimes discourage the artist from seeking the creation of new forms, nature is more of a limitation of the means of expression for aesthetic values, and this produces a disturbing contrast between the work of art and the feelings it wished to translate. The artist undertakes to transcend the kind of impotency read on the face of nature which makes contemplation ambiguous and makes us oscillate between melancholy and the birth of hope. It is the infinity of the artist's desire which does not succeed in mastering technical resources, in making them pliable and docile to its design. There follows the dissatisfaction which unceasingly incites the creator to obtain through new works of art a more complete reciprocal adaptation of forms, structures, and feelings whose signs they are. However, the unsuccessful work of art falls outside the area of what is capable of arousing emotion. It breaks the link it should have maintained with pure intention. It does not simply overturn it while maintaining it, as does fault.

One knows well enough that progress in truth is linked to resistance, which it occasions and permits us to define, resistance which makes us want to classify all resistance as refractory and hostile nature. Error is the consequence of this. But what is privative in it keeps us from confusing it with the being of a countervalue. Error invites transcendence and rehabilitation. It is also the support without which thought could not advance. Recognized and rejected, error dissolves. It does not so much usurp the place of truth as it leads toward it and serves it by gropings and endless adjustments. It does not compound itself as does fault. If it were permissible to distinguish between the nontrue and the false, one could say that the false is the hardening of error and that it does not so much announce truth as it betrays it or opposes its advancement. The false has its own consistency, and one must break with it as with vice.

In this way, finally, is revealed the unique meaning of the values of existence and action. What we grasp in them, what we qualify by them, is the generative process of the being of the self. It is, identically, the act of being and the act of being worthwhile, the act of not being and the act of not being worthwhile. Here there is—and there is no other example—the influence in the being of the self of an intention which did not aim directly at the growth of the self but at action in its intrinsic quality. However, in thus reflecting on the self, action discerns a relationship between pure consciousness and real consciousness which must remain masked as long as the process is being accomplished. It seems that the self can be worthwhile only insofar as it acts. Further, it cannot act without recreating through action itself the difference which separates it from its being and from the principle which makes it be.

BOOK III
Existence

6 / Theory Concerning Inclination

AT THIS POINT we will not pretend to ignore the certitude attained by the self reflecting on its past. Nor will we avoid introducing this certitude into the development of the self within the world. At the height of reflection, real consciousness cannot be assured of its real relationship to pure consciousness without the feeling it has of itself, in action and in effort, being interiorly modified. Nevertheless, the very character of this relationship requires not only that the self be spared no trial but that there be no moment in which the self could imagine that it had effected this relationship. Furthermore, philosophical consciousness of this relationship cannot constitute a privilege or create in a man the illusion that he is more advanced than his fellow wayfarers along the road of existence or that he witnesses to this philosophical consciousness better than they do. In fact, reflection leaves the self at the very point from which it started. The conditions which decide the promotion of the being of the self cannot be deduced from its deep certitude. Other minds can ignore the relationship of their existence to their true being without their superiority being less striking or the advance of their existence less certain. However, instead of being surprised by this, consciousness should rather see in it proof of the authenticity of a relationship which can be verified only in an indirect manner through practical goals.

It follows that the relationship of real consciousness to pure consciousness would be strongly confirmed if the spontaneous expansion of the self revealed that the self is motivated by a desire in which one might rightly judge that this relationship

[85]

shone through in the only way possible for it to become efficacious in a being which is directed by tendencies and which acts
only in view of goals. But what desire? In the midst of desires
expressing natural tendencies, what sign can help one distinguish a desire in which tendencies would be included, to which
tendencies contribute their force, and which, nevertheless, as a
desire, is not one of these tendencies or even the totality of
them? No question is more decisive for the development of real
consciousness. This amounts to asking whether it is possible for
the self to still be interested in itself once it no longer defines
itself by its inclinations but according to possibilities of existence not inscribed to its given nature.

To what should we relate a desire which comes from no
particular tendency but which would reject no one of them as
radically incompatible with itself? To what should we relate a
desire whose satisfactions are not to be confused with the satisfactions of natural tendencies but which appropriate these tendencies, a desire which neither the weakening nor the decay of
tendencies would exhaust and which has need of these tendencies only to borrow from them a very weak strength without
giving away any of its own strength? No inclination of nature
corresponds to this desire, even though all inclinations are sub-
missive to it. This desire would then express an inclination
which, at first, might be as unconscious of itself as are originally
unconscious the inclinations of nature which attain self-awareness only in objects they desire and in the emotions they arouse.
This pure inclination would affirm its presence by calling forth
and by favoring goals capable of rerouting natural tendencies
and instincts away from their original object or destination. Just
as instincts and tendencies allow the satiety of desire to last
only for a moment, so likewise this pure inclination is satisfied
only for an instant by the success of goals which transcend those
of nature. However, if this pure inclination became conscious of
itself through the very renewal of its desire, it would not avow
itself dependent on the object of the goals to which it lent itself.

Would not all the characteristics of this inclination be those
which an inclination would have to possess for a self, whose
being is defined by a twofold relationship to pure consciousness
and to a given nature, to force itself to be equal to itself? Should
one be surprised that this inclination remains masked by instincts? How could it be otherwise if this inclination must in

some way live off these instincts, nourishing itself on their substance, and if, in order to be fully equal to its own exigencies, it must weaken natural tendencies? If one were to require this pure inclination, in the desire to be in which it expresses itself, to be capable of breaking all ties with tendencies, even of being opposed to them and of dominating them, must one forget that one would succeed in doing so only by relying on these tendencies and by rediscovering them at a higher level, where they are more susceptible of sustaining and nourishing an aspiration which transcends them?

Is not this pure inclination, this desire to be, a fiction? Can one ask human experience to witness to its presence? Nothing could be less demonstrative. Every evidence of human experience remains fundamentally equivocal. No matter what heights human morality were to attain, it could always manage to consider its successes as the extension of the spontaneous expansion of tendencies. No matter how mediocre the level at which human morality establishes itself, one can always manage to discover there the trace of an aspiration not found in nature. Just as there is reason to reject every definition of man which would shut him up in a concept and all humanism which would remain at the level of man, even if conceived as indefinite extension of his powers, so there is reason to reject an abstract supernaturalism which parallels the actual course of history with an illusory spiritualism. What most often happens? When one condemns natural inclination, one does so in the name of an aspiration which seems unceasingly to be obstructed by this natural inclination. But when, from the very beginning, one adopts this natural inclination, one considers that one finds in the spontaneity of its *élan* the force and the source of a flowering of the self which in the end turns against the original instinct. Unsociability becomes love of another, aspiration to happiness becomes devotion, will to power becomes suppression of self and sacrifice. One forgets that consciousness can free itself from inclination only by borrowing its causality and that it can give way to inclination only by lending it its light.

On the other hand, one must understand correctly the true meaning of a pure, practical teleology, in the Kantian sense, that is, of a moral theory constructed in such a way that the principles of action cannot be suspected of taking their value from the tendencies of the empirical will. This pure moral teleology

shunts aside the pretension of natural tendencies to offer themselves as such to a pure will. It is a necessary moment in all
study to determine the principles and goals of a pure will while
maintaining the duality of moral goals and those goals which
issue from nature. However, if moral rationalism made of this
moment the whole of an ethic, it would prevent itself from
aiding, as it can, the dialectic of aspiration which is the dialectic
of existence itself. Even in the most rigorous rationalism of
Kant, one recognizes many traces of an effort not to separate
completely pure will and sensibility. One recognizes an effort to
relate pure practical teleology to anthropology without erasing
the opposition between what is pure and what is "pathological."
It is necessary for moral law to be willed by a subject. There is
no study more important than that which concerns the pure
motives of morality. Such study requires one to conceive the will
as determined by immediate interest in the law seen as a pure
attraction exercised by reason on the subject. Undoubtedly, this
interest has nothing of sensibility in it; it expresses the immediate effect of the representation of law on a consciousness. It is
no less true that it is what is subjective in this pure motivation
that makes reason efficacious and brings it into a real will. On
the other hand, one does not ignore the fact that the establishment of a pure teleology is necessarily completed by a study of
the conditions of possibility of the realization of the goals of a
real will in the world.

Beginning with the idea of a pure will, what appeared as the
production of an interest exempt from all sensual attraction is,
in another sense, a conversion which, taking place within natural
desire, does not so much destroy or combat natural desire as it
makes it docile for goals originally not its own. Nevertheless,
just as there is no reason to seek to explain the production of a
pure interest in morality in a rigorously rationalist conception of
the law, so there is no possibility of explaining the conversion
which takes place within desire. It is a conversion which permits
a pure inclination to break through, an inclination capable of
obtaining from nature and in nature, in harmony with the tendencies of man, participation in the pursuit of goals not found in
nature. The crisis in which the conversion of desire is an-
nounced and accomplished is distinct, and must remain distinct,
from that which a psychologist might undertake to describe in
an effort to throw light on the development of the empirical life

of the will. In a general way, the question posed here is nothing less than that of the passage of the consciousness of a being who is in a given inescapable relationship with himself to the consciousness of a being capable of breaking this relationship. However, for the psychologist, who follows and describes the history of consciousness, the rupture of this relationship is no different from any other moment in which nothing more would be in question than a sort of pause, an interruption or a hesitation, in the expansion of an instinct, thanks to which this instinct could subsequently direct itself more surely toward the object of its desire. The nonempirical origin of this rupture or of this conversion can be established only to the extent that one can establish that it is the condition of possibility of a dialectic of aspiration capable of bringing the self closer to its being and of carrying it to the level expected of it by the pure generative intentions of value. However, it is this dialectic itself which alone can offer proof of its possibility and of the authenticity of the acts which constitute it.

In the beginning, all we can hope for is to surprise the nonnecessary moment which marks the advent of existence for self and opens up an indefinite career for the creation of self by deciding on a new collaboration between consciousness and inclination. If this moment is decisive, it will manifest itself as the condition of possibility of later acts in which the overturning of the original relationship between consciousness and inclination will be accomplished. In man, deep unawareness of his natural soul is joined at first to consciousness of desire and to representation of the object capable of satisfying it. The real causality of inclination cannot be revealed to consciousness whose attention is riveted on the object. Consciousness is literally outside of itself because, first of all, it has no way of grasping directly the energy of inclination at work. Inclination does not disclose its secret in the images in which desire is determined, in the suffering which characterizes the withdrawal from possession, in the restlessness, mixed with pleasure, which anticipates success. Refracted in emotions, in dreams, in the observations which accompany desire, inclination becomes less transparent since it is as if covered over by the inner discourse of a consciousness which does not know that what it thinks hides from it what it is.

Could an objective knowledge of inclination free the self? Could such knowledge make consciousness be something other than simply a prism in which instinct is reflected? Undoubtedly, with an explicative hypothesis one could relate representations and behavior to inclination interpreted as a cause or a force. This way one would account for the kind of fabulation which is grafted onto the play of instinct. However, this knowledge of inclination finally presents no interest for a concrete consciousness to which objective knowledge offers an image of itself in which it does not recognize itself, in which it can find no help for reform and possession of self. The original servitude of consciousness with respect to inclination does not make it dependent on inclination in the way that an effect is dependent on its condition. There is no determinism here from which knowledge might free one or which one might be permitted to utilize. Nor is it in pretending to dismiss inclination that consciousness frees itself. This is why knowledge of objective determinism leaves it either indifferent or miserable.

If the original relationship of consciousness to inclination places consciousness in a state of radical dependence on inclination and maintains it in a state of unawareness, this is because only in the interval which separates desire from satisfaction does consciousness awaken to itself. Consciousness awakens only to the extent that, cut off from the object which calms desire, it is born and dies as often as resistance and delays arise and disappear—resistance interior to the acting being, and delays which issue from the world with which instinct is solidary. Consciousness must define itself as the experience of separation. It is such at the starting point; it remains such until the end of its history. However, this separation radically changes meaning as the effort of the self to be equal to itself is put forth. The dialectic of aspiration is constructed out of the overturning of this experience. At the level of inclination, action is destined to bring closer and to hasten the moment of satisfaction. This satisfaction is no sooner experienced than consciousness is astonished, without understanding it, that it is impossible to exhaust the energy of the tendency otherwise than by means of objects which deceive consciousness as much as they satisfy it. However, for a self which aspires to produce itself, action becomes the unique way to verify both that it draws closer to its being and that at the same time it always remains distant from that being.

Still, no matter how humble, how ephemeral at first, is the

feeling of contrast between the depth of inclination and the satisfaction obtained after the tendency has, in a way, been projected outside of itself in search of the object, this feeling is the condition of possibility, as well as the index of a consciousness in which a desire is born which is no longer identified with the desire directed to and dependent on the object. It is a consciousness which comes to knowledge of itself only in the interval which separates it from the object. It acquires knowledge of itself through the resistance which it encounters and the inner tension which accompanies it. This desire, which awakens in the depths of desire, is evidence of the fact that consciousness, which was only the experience of a certain opposition which it had both to undergo and surmount, does not return to nothingness. In order to illuminate the tendency, this desire uses the light it receives from the resisted expansion of inclination. To illuminate the tendency is no longer to be subject to the law which subordinates the tendency, and subordinates consciousness of it, to the acquisition of an object which remains in some way exterior to it. To illuminate the tendency is to bring the tendency back to itself; it is, at the same time, to put it at the service of a goal capable of satisfying an aspiration to be in which a self is enunciated which is no longer identified with inclination alone. Once it is no longer a prisoner of the relationship between inclination and object, desire becomes another kind of desire; love declares itself, and also renunciation. One might doubt that subjectivity, linked to the initial curiosity of inclination, is at all different from the impatience of delayed desire. But the curiosity of inclination at work accepts a limitation which in some way plays the role of a nonself in relationship to inclination. The dialectic of aspiration gravitates around this opposition. The subjectivity which is produced to calm this opposition cannot do so except by appropriating inclination for a goal which it is called to serve, even though this goal transcends it. Here is revealed this paradox in an ethic: that the roots of inclination must never be cut, that the sap of inclination must circulate within goals most distant from the primary function of the tendency.

In the last analysis, the contingent determination, the initial limitation of an inclination imprisoned by contacts which left desire dependent on the world, would be converted into a choice of liberty. However, this conversion of consciousness to itself can fully be realized only by a reconquest of inclination, and this in turn cannot be accomplished without inclination being emptied of its substance. This conversion is verified first of all by a transformation for existence of the meaning of the dimensions of time. As long as desire is, in fact, subject to the law of the object, whose contact and possession it seeks and anticipates, it is also subject to the constraint of a time which forces it to distribute its moments along the interval to be traversed. Consciousness experiences a contrast which remains mysterious to it. It is a contrast between the future in which its desire is projected and the passing of time, which slips by it to the extent that its desire is eaten up in some way by an impatient but impotent desire. Consciousness has no true present in the sense that each of the moments in which the thought of desire is manifested offers the same contrast between a future which consciousness anticipates and a present which is only the contraction of an interval which disappears immediately into the past. For consciousness its own history is only the vestige of its waiting. But the overturning of the relationship of consciousness to desire and the appropriation of inclination which follows upon it begin at once to transform the value of the dimensions of time. These contract into a present in which the generative law of a future is created unceasingly for consciousness. Consciousness works to constitute this future instead of depending on it. The future of consciousness does not so much draw closer to consciousness as it is the field consciousness opens up in order to return to itself. Consciousness gathers in its past in order to rely on it. New feelings are compensation for this conversion produced within inclination. What interest it has for action is not overlooked; all the warmth of the most natural feelings, those nearest to instinct, is preserved. But there is no longer any fear, deception, or betrayal which can restrict inclination to itself and make it prisoner of its object.

Thus defined, the dialectic of aspiration must successively arouse all the crises in which are decided, in both the history of humanity and the history of each self, the concrete relationships between nature and a desire, an inclination, which transcends nature. However, up until now we have pretended to consider natural inclination as simple or as one; we have not taken into account the plurality and the diversity of tendencies. Must the unity of aspiration lend itself to the diversity of tendencies, or must the diversity of tendencies lend itself to the unity of aspiration? The relationships between natural inclination and aspiration can only appear here under a new aspect. If the many satisfactions, if the objects sought by instinct, had not divided instinct and accentuated its virtual diversity, and if inclination had remained within itself, one would not remark so much its opposition to the unity of the desire to be. But the spontaneous expansion of inclination multiplied the limitations to which it was subject and intensified its inner diversity in such a way that the conversion of inclination seemed destined to introduce or to restore a new unity there. The dialectic of aspiration is now produced in the presence of tendencies which seem to rival one another or to be impenetrable to one another. The separation of these seems to be aggravated, if not produced, by the subservience of inclination to the object and to the world. Fascinated again and again by different objects, consciousness seems to spread itself out in tendencies which no longer seem to be expressions or variations of a fundamental inclination.

From this point of view, one can understand, it seems, the *raison d'être* for the effort by many doctrines of naturalistic inspiration to reduce the diversity of tendencies and to substitute for this diversity the simplicity and the unity of an original tendency. These doctrines do not proceed, as they claim, from observation of facts and human nature or even essentially from a theoretical exigency, from the exigency of understanding directing itself toward a unitary explanation of behavior. It is evident that the concern for explanation is dominated in them by the attempt to link a philosophy of action to theoretical or objective knowledge. Using the science of man, it is an effort to illuminate action in such a way that man, beneath all the changes which social life or any other cause might effect in the original movement of inclination, would want what he already wanted and what he cannot cease wanting once he comes back to himself. This question is nothing less than that of resting the *terminus ad quem* which every philosophy of action secretly envisions on a *terminus a quo* furnished by nature. Since it is impossible to deny the deep desire of the self, which is desire of unity, the initial unity of the tendency seems the surest way to give foundations to the unity which action and morality seek to realize. Then it would only be a question of rediscovering the original tendency, of giving it full self-consciousness as well as consciousness of its direction. Just as hope often expresses itself by belief in a past golden age, so the unity envisioned and desired becomes, retroactively, the naturalistic unity of an inclination which allowed itself to fall into disunity and which has strayed from its deep desire.

The naturalistic interpretation of man through the unity of a fundamental tendency would thus seem to lend itself to a description of human experience which in many points would coincide with that given by philosophers inspired by opposite principles: the same blindness, the same ignorance of consciousness with respect to its essential desire, the same dissolution of the tendency, the same orientation of the whole being toward the possession of self. It is the surpassing of inclination that one hopes to obtain through the metamorphoses of inclination. It is so for the tendency to perseverance in being, for self-love, for the tendency to satisfaction, for the will to power. Without leaving inclination, it is something like a displacement of inclination that one anticipates. In the context of a naturalistic monism, admitted in principle, one anticipates a liberation from nature itself.

However, the natural unity of inclination can only be an explanatory hypothesis which will always have against it the fact of the apparent plurality of tendencies and objects which satisfy it. On the other hand, the teleological unity of inclination would mark the achievement of an aspiration which finds in the disaccord of tendencies the opposition by which it gets hold of itself in the guise of a desire which does not have its source in nature. The more one is inclined to affirm the unity of a primitive inclination, which one must admit became divided against itself, the more one must be brought to consider that the teleological unity of a will, which imitates the unity of primitive inclination, nevertheless has to this inclination a purely superficial resemblance whose foundation is different.

From outside, nothing permits us to distinguish the exercise of a will which is already outside of life from the exercise of a will which is prisoner of instinct, unless it be instinct itself. Only consciousness can undertake to learn whether the energy of its will and the quality of its feelings issue from an attachment to life as such or to a goal which wants to consume this life. The whole problem comes back, then, to seeking the conditions of possibility for an integration of tendencies by means of an aspiration which is at once similar and contrary to the original unity of inclination. If these conditions exist, if they permit the appropriation of tendencies for a goal other than themselves, these conditions will be at the same time proof of an inclination which does not have any strength itself but which makes both constitutive relations of our being participate in one another: relationship to life, on the one hand, and to a pure consciousness, on the other hand.

The question would have to receive a negative answer if there were integration of tendencies only by subordination of all to one or by their harmonious development and the reciprocal aid which they would offer each other without necessary recourse to anything but nature. But the problem changes meaning if these tendencies can contrive, without internal rivalry, to serve a goal which was inscribed in no one of them but which is nevertheless capable of rallying and guiding all of them to collaborate in a vision which transcends nature. It is a case of a goal issuing from an idea which is incommensurable with the goals implied in tendencies but which appropriates these tendencies and directs their energies to its service. If there were not a formal resemblance between the way in which an idea, which has arisen from an act of consciousness, tends at once to order to itself and to capture all the elements it needs for organizing itself into a creative process and the way in which a tendency rooted in organic life unfolds by attracting to itself sympathetically the forces capable of aiding it, one would not understand that pure ideas can be so powerful in souls. Every idea, despite what it represents of an infinite exigency, must borrow the form of a concrete goal, not only for self-assurance in the midst of the world, but also for appropriation of tendencies involved in a process of analogous form. It does this by bringing these inclinations back from the object in which they lose themselves to the aspiration which they are going to serve.

While natural inclination can obtain self-satisfaction only by becoming dependent on the object, while it can be assured of the complicity of other tendencies only by doing violence to them, the idea frees inclination from nature while at the same time placing nature at its disposal. The goal in which it unfolds sets in motion an aspiration which expects nothing from the world even though it can realize itself only with the complicity of the world. In willing what it did not will, the tendency receives what it would have anticipated in vain from the possession of its natural object. Ambition, self-love, the will to power are forgotten, efface themselves, in favor of the goal born of the idea. They obtain by this renunciation a pure satisfaction which is still the satisfaction of ambition, of self-love, of the will to power. The unity of the idea, through the exigency of totalization which is proper to it, produces a coordination, an integration, among tendencies which no natural object would have been capable of realizing.

One can find evidence for this in the harmony of satisfactions which experience shows is either impossible from the single point of view of nature or so precarious that without fail it leaves behind it nostalgia for another world in which we do not know how to subsist when chance has led us there. The incompatibility of satisfactions is one of the signs of the rivalry and plurality of tendencies. This incompatibility is a sign, first of all, because each of these tendencies is dependent on contact with an object whose accord with the tendency presents a high degree of fortuitousness and inadequacy. It is a sign, in the second place, because each of these objects responds to a vision which occupies the whole soul only by arousing a kind of self-discontent and remorse by complacency in an inclination which includes some kind of treason with respect to a nonsatisfied desire for totality. The case is different when the self is fused with the goal of an idea whose object is not imposed on it by nature. It is not even the success of this goal that is here a reason for satisfaction. Much more, by a sort of compensation, the reason for satisfaction is a facility, a confluence of all satisfactions linked to spontaneous tendencies. It is as if, by collaborating in a goal which transcends them, these tendencies are reconciled. If ambition, combativeness, and love conspire and lose themselves in some way in dedication to a goal which was not given or prefigured in any of the movements of nature; if in return for this dedication, without their having sought or anticipated such a reward, these tendencies acquire, each for itself, a new signification and depth, making each feeling participate in the unity and in the totalization realized in the soul by a will which remains beyond each of them; if nature is thus totally recollected by the very effect of the decision which at first seemed to deny it or dominate it, it is an indication that an integration of inclination is accomplished by an aspiration, by a pure inclination, which does not belong to nature. It follows that nature rediscovers its purity and allows us to consent to material satisfactions only on the condition that we have begun to constitute ourselves through a will and a desire which are beyond all satisfactions.

One fundamentally misunderstands the dialectic of aspiration when one conceives of an action against the tendencies which could be conducted directly, as if the struggle against the tendencies constituted an end in itself. One likewise misunderstands the dialectic of aspiration when one expects from some unknown spontaneous sublimation of tendencies a conversion of the tendency to an order which transcends it. There is as much difference between a dream in which desire plays its role and a work of art whose planning and realization mobilize all the forces of the individual. On the other hand, the discipline of tendencies fails if one attempts to secure it by repression and by constraint exercised on the instinct. Even though partially efficacious, this discipline would gradually deprive existence of all force and of all sap by reducing morality to consciousness of a law. It would be difficult to see how this consciousness of law would be able to make itself loved and willed.

What is specious in the theory of the conversion of a means into an end, even its radical insufficiency in the face of the problem of the integration of tendencies, is also discovered this way. If it is correct that, although initially servants of a natural ambition, certain activities, requiring the discipline of thought as much as patience or courage, acquire an intrinsic value which both frees them from all subordination to a goal whose condition they were and elevates them well beyond that goal; if, in this way, one can attempt to conceive the genesis of higher values, it seems that this can only be a first step toward the integration of tendencies. One must add to it a radical conversion by which the order of subordination of these activities and these tendencies is overturned. It is in coming to serve, after having commanded, that tendencies obtain by this very fact an unexpected quality and cooperate in the unity of the self.

Thus, truthfully speaking, it is not means which becomes an end, but it is, with the cooperation of means, the discovery of a method, the creation of a goal which transcends nature, although the attempts which preceded it may have hastened the advent of this goal. There is a moment when the technique of instinct gives way to a creation which submits instinct to its hegemony and makes it participate in the promotion of the order of beauty and truth. Seeking to share in some desired object, so that the acquisitive instinct of each may be satisfied, men discover and invent an order of justice which surprises them because subsequently it regulates instinct and their actions, because this order of justice has a constant value, indifferent to the suggestions and the partiality of desire. From that moment on, the permanence of the direction which imposes on feeling the maintenance or the promotion of a goal, creative of its own object, contradicts the intermittence of emotions, which reflect the vicissitudes of desire. The hegemony of this goal is not comparable to the hegemony of a tendency. It is creative of the unity of a self which wills itself totally in terms of this goal, while the idea from which the goal issues proposes an infinite task to the self. It is true to say that in the widest sense morality begins with the production of a goal whose intrinsic regulation no longer is jointly dependent on desire and on the world.

If resistance arises, consciousness no longer suffers from it in the same way it suffered from the resistance which exacerbated its desire. The appropriation of tendencies and their integration by a goal which ideally expresses the relationship of real consciousness to pure consciousness are never so complete that they allow natural inclination to manifest in any other way than by transparency the pure inclination which it sets in motion. Just as the mastery which we exercise over our life must be willing to realize itself through inclinations of which none is such that it does not bind us to work in the world and to relations we contract with other beings, so it cannot be that all rivalry would be entirely wiped out between the goal of an organizing will, dependent on an idea which does not belong to nature, and the goal of tendencies. Besides, if we are denied all the conditions for a flowering of the tendencies themselves, for ambition and for love, we are in great part deprived of the means of discerning and experiencing, within satisfactions enjoyed by these tendencies, the quality of satisfaction of another order. But disappointment, linked to the fact that the idea generative of a pure goal must be realized with the help of inclinations, works to have us grasp the difference between the incessant oscillation from satisfaction to disappointment, which is the law of a tendency which remains at the level of natural tendencies, and the feeling in which the invincible disparity between pure aspiration and the goal which expresses it is manifested.

While aspiration invites us to an integration of tendencies through a goal which would have all movements of the soul working together, while the self would like to realize in a single act the signification of the idea and exhaust it within that act, it is most often necessary for the self to identify its will with a goal which does not succeed in appropriating and in rallying all the force of tendencies. The rational form of a law by which liberty is determined must complement the identity of liberty and of a goal which would succeed in excluding none of the desires welling up unceasingly from the depths of the inclinations of nature. It is necessary, it is inevitable, for the aspiration, in which the relationship of real consciousness to primary certitude is revealed, to mask itself and give way before duty and the law, as long as the pure intention, from which this aspiration issues, and the force of inclinations, which it is destined to weaken, are not enveloped in a single creative goal. This operation fills in all the space between the initial dissolution of desire and serenity.

7 / Ascesis through Goals

IF INTEGRATION of the inclinations of nature reveals to oneself an aspiration whose development is identified with the development of existence, it also brings one to the threshold of a new problem. Integration does not yet allow one to determine the relationship between goals, in view of which the will acts in conformity with this aspiration, and values it would like to promote through these goals. Not only is the goal of pure will not identified with the aspiration at the heart of this will, not only does this goal necessarily control a diversity of goals in which the bond which they have with pure will is slackened, but all these goals together are sought for themselves and not for the value affecting the action which produces them. Values are the modes in which a real consciousness in its commerce with the world verifies its own relationship to pure consciousness. But this verification can be made only indirectly by means of goals and tasks for which the will acts. At the source of creation in every order there is an intention which is turned not toward itself but away from itself. This intention can detect itself only in an operation already begun, in the outline of a task, in the goal toward which the will is directed. The first thrust of all creation is, literally, a project in which at first the intention denies itself and remains unknown to itself. However, through the project it has a chance, if not to return to itself and to its inner act, at least to experience its relationship to the generative intention of value. Neither love nor courage nor holiness can be sure of itself unless it is enveloped in goals which borrow all

[100]

their substance from the world. But what proportion, what correlation, is there between these goals and values?

One notices first of all that this correlation between goals and values is often so imperfect that it can induce consciousness to attempt a kind of disassociation between them. It can tempt consciousness to become uninterested in the advancement of morality in the world through goals. The temptation is to withdraw into the pure interiority of a willing, of an energy entirely applied to maintaining itself by its own perfection. Or consciousness withdraws into a concentration of thought that is attentive to emptying itself of all that is born of its commerce with the world so that it may better turn itself toward the principle which illuminates it. To a lesser extent, it is the exaltation of an intention assuring itself of the quality of its inner action. In all cases, there is a certain depreciation of goals. Either one considers goals as purely symbolic of a willing which we have more chance of approaching in an entirely inner action, or one considers goals as fundamentally contingent in relationship to intentions generative of values, or one considers goals as relative to a world, society, and relationships between things and persons about which there is no reason to think that they directly concern our possibilities of existence. More deeply, it is the feeling that the pursuit of these goals leaves parts of our being undeveloped and that it cannot save us. Suppose one consents to recognize these goals. Often this leads to maintaining them on a level inferior to an experience of another order which no longer belongs, it is believed, to what concerns an ethic, properly speaking. Since there is, in fact, a second experience which duplicates our experience within the world and suggests to us that this life does not disclose the secret of existence or that in it we remain separated from our true being, we can be inclined to think that it would be possible to directly intensify this second experience by deliverance from the sensible world and by renunciation of goals which everything invites us to pursue.

On the other hand, considering the very definite opposition between values and goals which arises from the nature of goals in situations from which the will cannot disengage itself without betraying powerful moral interests, and ascertaining, in other cases, all the resources of moral energy expended in the service of detestable or reprehensible goals, one comes to think that it might be possible to separate values and goals so that the will, becoming indifferent to the goals, would concentrate on values.

How can one not also be astonished by the kind of disproportion often manifested between goals sought by the will and values which shine forth in action and affect the person? Goals lack brilliance and, modest as they are, can barely enter into the system of moral ends; values shine forth all the more, the lower goals are. In many circumstances, there seems to be a moral substance of the person, independent of what he does, and without relationship, one might say, to the degree one might assign to the goals of his will in the hierarchy of ends. What the person is and what he is worth seem to have no common measure with what he accomplishes. At least love knows this well, for it does not judge on merit and is not discouraged by contrary evidence or disaccord between goals and the quality of beings. The very fact that certain qualities radically escape the will which would like to acquire them directly, reinforces the idea of an independence of values from goals. At least this is so if one grants that values have this characteristic of being separable from pure intentions and from the growth of being or of existence for the self. On this point of view hangs the defense of a legitimate indifference of consciousness to all goals which appear incompatible with certain values or value intentions. One turns away from the goals of social life or the goals of the political order because only with difficulty are they reconciled with the values of purity and sincerity which consciousness esteems above all. If it is the nature of certain goals, solidary with the nature of social groups, social milieux, and means used, to be pursued only by endangering certain values at the same time, consciousness will decide to stay away from these goals. If all the goals of the immanent order together truly give way in the face of a supreme goal, the will, which aims at this supreme goal in a pure movement of charity, will undoubtedly accomplish the goals of the immanent order. It will do so, however, in addition and as a task to which it gives itself, not because it recognizes in this task any intrinsic significance but because in the present life it will be the closest it can come to working symbolically for possession of what is uniquely necessary.

These first difficulties, the diversity of attitudes of consciousness which correspond to them, and the doctrines whose expression one sees they are, already enunciate how the relationship between values and goals touches a desire to be and to be worthwhile which cannot have itself as a goal or consider itself as an object without at once discovering the vanity of its attempt. By definition the generative intention of value gives value only indirectly by investing in an action in which this intention loses and forgets itself by willing the action as such in its intrinsic significance. This is true in all orders. In the interests of a self which wants to be worthwhile, even when it is a question of qualities which do not seem to depend so much on action as on the most interior and spontaneous movements of consciousness, consciousness must not direct its attention to these movements but must remain, above all, open to the world and to other minds.

Thus only abstractly is it correct to disassociate in the quality of an action or of a being what belongs to the value intention from what belongs to the goal without which this intention remains empty. However, what is the true nature of the bond which unites them and of the tension between them, which in our experience never completely disappears? Could not their apparent correlation be the expression of a deeper identity, of an identity getting hold of itself from two different points of view?

It seems that this is what would have to happen in a world, in a nature, penetrated by finality if, beneath the determinism by which it lends itself to science, it was worked through by an aspiration which makes it tend toward a higher intelligibility and toward a consciousness of this intelligibility through the progress of beings themselves, or if, in whatever way you might wish, it was growth and production of an order which prolonged and expressed itself in the creation of forms of social life most propitious for exalting relations between minds. Once the goals of human behavior are attuned to the finality of the universe which they unfold, once these goals take root in this finality which they are called to promote and absorb into consciousness of self, they are what, properly speaking, becomes value. These goals correspond to the moment in which a finality, still diffuse or hesitant in the universe or ignorant of itself, contracts in consciousness and there acquires its sense of direction. Instead of being the reflection on our actions, on our task, on our very beings of a position or a creation of consciousness superior to all nature, value is nothing more than the character of the goals which life assigns to itself, or rather they are the evidence of its ascending movement. From this point of view, one might say, an obscure desire to be worthwhile, in its humblest form, accompanies the progress of reality itself. This desire distinguishes itself from the progress of reality only to reflect on it and, after that, if it can, to go beyond it. But value comes to goals from nowhere else but from the goals themselves or from the nature from which these goals issue. Value does not add itself to reality. The way in which reality affects itself when it becomes conscious of self, of its source, or of the origin of its operations and of its progress is to be worthwhile. Thus, in a universe in which finality reigns everywhere, value is interior to this finality, to the goals in which it shares itself, goals which are just so many directions of its effort. It is interior to beings which borrow from this finality the movement and the aspiration which animate them. The desire to be or to be worthwhile, if it awakens in these beings, does not have to seek outside itself for goals to satisfy it. The value intention, in its highest form, will only duplicate in consciousness a process interior to reality itself. Between goals and values there is no true correlation, nor, even less, tension or opposition, but rather identity considered from different points of view.

The aim here has been only to indicate one of the directions that might be taken by an ethic careful to seek its foundation nowhere but in the immanent spontaneity of the totality of the real. Ideal goals, the goals of an ethic, are thus most real in the sense of unfolding, in consciousness and for the will which appropriates them, an aspiration which elevates and moves nature. One can see very well in this respect what happens to liberty in its relationship to values and goals. If liberty is an element of value, it is such to the extent that it is a spontaneity creative of goals which illuminates itself and becomes conscious of self. Liberty does not insert in the value an intention which transcends nature and which the goals are called to serve.

It is otherwise if the desire to be or to be worthwhile transfers to a real consciousness, and to a self solidary with nature, its relationship to a source which does not belong to nature. But quite evidently, consciousness can neither verify nor directly promote this desire, as obscure as it first is to itself, by actions which would carry it to the level of the source which engenders it. The experience which consciousness has of its separation from itself forbids it, in its effort to return to itself, to aim at the source which keeps it from being once for all in a settled relationship to itself. There is no possible regression of its own genesis which would diminish the inequality of the relationship by which it is defined. Its desire to be worthwhile is already action, perhaps still entirely interior but having, nevertheless, a prospective character. Every attempt to force access to self directly is thus condemned, just as is all hope of a movement of consciousness toward self which would actually be a return to its source. There is no possible assimilation between the reflective inquiry which leads consciousness to assure itself about its source, to affirm it primarily, and its real action on the historical level with which all value begins and ends. The experience of delay which we have with respect to ourselves becomes an impatience to be, i.e., to be, now, in actions which verify as much as possible the certitude which makes us be. What is in our power, therefore, is to bring this experience of separation and its verification, that is, our desire itself, to different levels, to different heights, into different registers.

It would be contradictory that we should have any chance of succeeding by aiming at goals which were the prolongation of tendencies and given in some fashion with them. Such goals would leave us prisoners of our nature. There would be nothing in them which could satisfy the self or reveal to it a desire neither defined nor limited by the desire of any of these tendencies. For a real will involved in the world, its desire to be and the operation by which it begins to be worthwhile are invincibly in correlation with goals which are not at all predetermined in the structure of tendencies with which this will is solidary. That these goals have to interpret these tendencies much more than constrain them is a sign that these goals cannot be attained without the complicity of the tendencies but that they are not indebted to them for the value by which they are characterized with respect to the desire which they satisfy. As close apparently as these goals are to the tendencies which they control, they are distinguished from them. These goals not only add satisfaction to the tendencies; they also add an irreducible quality which makes them share in an order which life did not contain and which enunciates a value intention.

However, this value intention could neither know itself, nor deepen itself, nor appreciate the satisfaction which it receives if it did not involve itself in goals whose exigencies it welcomes as it defines them and from which, in so doing, it receives indirectly a guarantee of its own authenticity. What, then, are these goals, these activities, fulfilling this twofold condition of borrowing from tendencies their strength but not their object, and of revealing to the self a possibility of existence in which its desire to be obtains satisfaction even though it must give way to goals and expect everything from them? These are goals which, in the widest sense, one can call cultural goals—and all, from the most humble to the most complex, involve some creation—whose object cannot be obtained unless the will submits itself to rules, to internal necessities, to a system of conditions which is determined by the intrinsic quality of the work done or envisioned. It is the task of these goals to introduce into movements of an acting being as well as into his thought, into the energy which he expends as well as into his intentions, an interior regulation which commands tendencies because it is itself commanded by the quality of the action or of the work to be produced or constructed. However, through the whole span, from the simplest techniques, from tasks accomplished together which require a joining of wills and some kind of contract which binds them, up to the creations of science and art, from elementary transformations which man makes nature undergo by work up to spiritual productions in which universes are created, all these include for the acting will the obligation to submit to a kind of interior schema which regulates and organizes its own operations. The creation of these schemata is contemporaneous with the creation of these goals: it perfects or complicates itself with them. But this creation is present from the first moment in which this self-renunciation of natural inclination and of life for something other than self is accomplished. Because of this, consciousness is surprised to be worthwhile and begins to feel that it is by turning away from itself that it has some chance of discovering the secret of its own being. It is this ascesis of inclination through goals which are no longer those of inclination which furnishes an ethic with the conditions of possibility of the highest forms of dedication of which man is capable. If an ethic cannot dispense with considering these cultural goals and, even more generally, premoral forms of effort, it is because it discovers there an ascesis without which nothing of what it asks on its own score from the will would be possible. The entire dialectic of aspiration hangs on this; all creation is enunciated in it and has its roots there. When generative intentions of value involve themselves in the goals of loyalty and sacrifice for the highest satisfaction of existence, they still lean on the premoral forms of an ascesis of inclination through goals which are already the sign of some creation.

Nevertheless, this ascesis of inclination through goals which are not given in nature is the awakening of a possibility of existence for the self. This ascesis frees in the self a desire to be, a desire to be worthwhile, which was unknown to itself and henceforth reveals itself to itself as solidary with activities which interpret inclination as much as they add to it. These activities commandeer the time of consciousness by instituting in its moments a solidarity, a duration in which the solidarity ruled by the moments of action is reflected. The self is henceforth inclined to identify its possibilities of existence with the intentions and movements directed toward these goals. They serve and arouse a desire to be which would not have gained self-consciousness without them. When these goals have awakened self-consciousness, they unceasingly stimulate it and do not allow it to fall below what they require of themselves in dedication and suffering. If consciousness cannot yet be attentive to the fact that in giving itself to these goals it subordinates itself to its own creations, at least it learns not to separate its judgment of self or the quality of its satisfactions from these goals. In this sense it is the totality of cultural goals, implying an ascesis of tendencies, which one must correlate with the actions of being worthwhile, with possibilities of existence in which, for a consciousness committed to the world, is already expressed, unequally and diversely, an aspiration which itself witnesses to its relationship to a creative power. All these goals are the translation of this aspiration in a world in which the resistance it encounters amplifies immeasurably what it meets in itself. When these goals appear to contradict tendencies, when they redirect the energies of tendencies to other objects, when they force tendencies to delay their satisfactions, it is not so much to destroy them radically as to make them permeable to an action of a desire which transcends them. If among these goals there are some which seem to repress tendencies rather than elevate them to their level, it is because these goals are relative to a state of human things where what is most urgent is first of all to put up a kind of barrier to hold back the instincts. Once these goals have to admit their powerlessness to interpret tendencies in the direction of our highest aspiration, the divorce which they provoke between the activity which they demand of man and his nature is such that consciousness becomes incapable of perceiving in these goals a safeguard for its own desire to be and to be worthwhile.

This correlation between possibilities of existence for the self and goals which transcend instinct and do not take their value from it accompanies the whole history of desire. Even if there were not specifically moral goals, an ethic would have to recognize the totality of these correlations. It would have to discern how they work together, how sometimes they run contrary to one another, how they begin to serve a tendency to satisfaction which is not the satisfaction of the inclination of nature. In this manner an ethic would already fulfill its function, which is to instruct consciousness about the true conditions of its happiness. This is because it will have to say that these goals, because of their quality, are more or less apt to favor the conversion and integration of inclination, the integration of tendencies. It will have to hierarchize, as much as it can, the possibilities of existence to which these goals correspond and which it creates in order then to satisfy them. Also, it will have to detect the moment in which the correlation is broken between the possibility of existence of the self and the goals which it pursues or which it is required to pursue.

This rupture is produced or tends to be produced in different ways, but always to the greatest damage of consciousness and in conditions of which an ethic is judge when it considers the interests of the total self. This happens, first of all, when goals are proposed to the self without encountering in it or succeeding in arousing in it a possibility of existence capable of rallying effectively the deepest tendencies of the self and of producing motivation for acts concordant with what is intrinsically called for by the goals. Should ideal goals, freely conceived by the human spirit, rather than rooted in the effective development of tasks and in the annexation of tendencies which they have worked over, presume excessively on the possibilities of existence of the self or of humanity taken in its totality, they will be marked by a kind of unreality because they have not been able to solicit in the self the desire to be which they were nevertheless destined to satisfy. Or, these ideal goals will not succeed in obtaining dedication of the self except at the price of denaturing motives and intimate movements of consciousness which those goals would certainly require. It is characteristic of an ascesis through goals—and this is why it interests an ethic—to require of the subject interior acts and a linking of these acts and motives appropriate to the intrinsic quality of these goals, actions, and tasks. In like manner the strength of science resides in the fact that its advance is a function of the acts of a subject, of a motivation for these acts which is nourished by nothing else than by truth, which is to be served. It is around these acts and through these acts that a possibility of existence for the self is constituted. But nothing is gained if, insofar as it is conceivable, goals are sought by interior acts which are in disaccord with the quality of the goals themselves.

At the level of an ethic properly speaking, it is the profound feeling of this difficulty which led Kant, in his defiance but not condemnation of inclination, to require for a pure will an absolute goal which was nothing else but reason itself, considered as pure matter in the subjects in which it was incarnated. Reason already had a similar function from the point of view of the form determinative of action and decision. This establishment of reason as an absolute goal simply duplicated for the will, considered as a power of acting for goals, what was already for it the source of determination and value. But the problem goes beyond that of the goals of liberty or of practical reason. It is prefigured in all the goals which constitute a possibility of existence for the self in correlation with acts and an interior motivation which agrees with them.

It also follows from this that, in another perspective, the correlation between the possibilities of existence of the self and goals is broken. This happens if these goals are not up to the measure of man, that is, to his possibilities of dedication, if they do not speak to the aspiration which is at the foundation of his being, if finally they touch only a part of his self and leave unexpressed, outside their grasp, a desire to be which they impoverish by limiting it to their own object. Then a goal degenerates rapidly into a pure technique, as happens every time a goal only requires of man some task which tends to compartmentalize his being into independent activities. From this moment on, no matter what aid this activity gave in the formation of the self in which there already appeared some trace of liberty, the risk is great that this activity will only arouse disgust for existence, which will manifest itself in its totality by an appeal directed to tendencies whose satisfactions are meant to furnish some compensation for the suppressed aspiration. This disgust will also manifest itself by a willingness on the part of the self to be accessible to all the seductions exercised on it by the most indeterminate ideal. Having had to give up finding the *raison d'être* of its goals, or rather having had to give up relating this *raison d'être* to its own desire to be, the self will dedicate itself to goals which its reason disavows. There are a passion for pleasure and a passion for adventure or action which are the twofold expression of a disequilibrium between the unemployed powers of the self and the goals of its activity or the qualities of these goals, that is, their value. After having obtained an initial collaboration of tendencies, after having awakened in the self a desire to be and an assurance of being worthwhile, after having made the self feel that there is satisfaction for this desire to be only if it renounces obtaining it directly, these goals, no matter how intrinsic the quality of each of them, do not succeed in responding to the desire to be of the total self. But, reciprocally, as soon as it is exalted or exacerbated, without consenting to become solidary with a goal capable of nourishing it and of regulating interiorly the movements of consciousness, this desire no longer knows how to distinguish itself from the subjectivity which is properly its contrary, unless it aims at a mystical beyond which is beyond all goals.

Thus, besides their intrinsic quality, the measure of the value of goals would be found in their capacity to give satisfaction integrally to an aspiration in which, for a real consciousness, is expressed the relationship constitutive of its being. But, strictly speaking, no goal can do this unless, to the ascesis which each of them spontaneously involves, there is added an ascesis which issues from the self itself, by means of which it renounces possibilities of existence of which it became aware because of these different goals. Here there appears a dimension characteristic of an ethic. After having considered in all the goals with intrinsic value and even in work itself, as the regulated action of man in nature, the contribution which they bring to the liberation of the self through the integration and conversion of inclinations, this ethic invites the self to choose itself. In order for the correlation between possibilities of existence and goals to excuse the self from this ascesis and to suppress the tension which arises between the former and the latter, it is not only necessary that the goals of liberty be fully in accord with the highest possibilities of existence of the self; it is also necessary for there to be a proportion between the level of the goals and the actions in which the desire to be must seek its deepest satisfaction. Further, it is necessary that each goal include in some way all the other goals or be able to substitute for these goals its own content and thus be capable of responding to the aspiration of the total self. However, not only the limitation of the strength of the self is opposed to this, but also the special character of goals and their quality.

It is not that an ethic can be indifferent to a deduction of the functions of creative consciousness and consequently to the value assignable to different goals. Nor does this ethic have to rule out the ideas of an ideal complementarity of these functions and their value. This complementarity would be susceptible of prolonging itself or of changing into a complementarity of activities of the self and of satisfactions. A sort of alternation might give, and in fact does give, to this complementarity the beginning of a concrete verification in an existence successively attentive to contemplation, knowledge of truth, participation in social life, friendship, and love. But finally this can only be a complementarity which remains in the order of enjoyment, not of doing. It is one which reveals itself inoperative when what is in question for a self is a test which must decide on its value, that is, on its being.

This solidarity, this agreement between goals and their value, is the equivalent of the Sovereign Good in modern consciousness, better instructed as to the autonomy of the creative functions of different universes in which it moves and of the provinces of the soul which correspond to them. There is nothing more legitimate, on the other hand, than to will that there be a proportion between the level of goals and actions, between the quality of goals and the quality of the act by which consciousness lends itself to them in order to be worthwhile. The progress of existence could be defined in this manner. Thus the scandal of a disharmony between the dedication of the self and the quality as well as the grandeur of causes should cease. It is right that this point of view guide thought in the constitution of a system of goals as well as in the determination of correlations between these goals and the possibilities of existence of the self. But, having said that, it is too evident that consciousness cannot wait for the realization of conditions for an accord between what it considers its deepest possibilities of existence and the quality of goals. It is the action of consciousness or its choice which will realize these conditions. For its part, consciousness cannot linger over this question without showing that it esteems itself before it has become worthwhile.

Therefore it is necessary to maintain inseparably both that the quality of goals, their level, and the grandeur of causes must not be indifferent to the desire to be worthwhile and that the accomplishment of the self can be attained by the most humble goals. In our judgment concerning the value of acts consideration of the historical weight of circumstances to which they are bound almost always intervenes. This is right, because these circumstances have been for the acting being an element in his decision. In them he learned to recognize the way to transcend himself. But the gift of self to goals which are not particularly distinguished, which shine in no particular way, or renunciation of other possibilities of existence in their favor, or the intensity of participation of the total being in these goals—these embody another point of view, which does not contradict the first but which is not to be identified with it, either. This limitation, this concentration, of possibilities of existence and, in measured degrees, this singular verification of desire in an action, task, or duty is the most characteristic moment of the ascesis of choice which is superimposed on the ascesis of inclination through goals. In the last analysis there is no value except at this price: that a correlation be realized between the possibilities of existence of a self and a goal participating in some manner through its quality in an order which transcends the tendencies of nature as such. This is not because an infinite objective would then express or incarnate itself in the finite. It is so because concrete consciousness has no other way of verifying an aspiration in which is manifested the relationship which it sustains with an unconditioned affirmation from which all intentions generative of value proceed.

Does liberty, whose history in a real consciousness accompanies, step by step, the dialectic of aspiration, now have content adequate to its idea? The integration of tendencies, the ascesis of inclination through goals, the birth of possibilities of existence for the self, the renunciation of many of these possibilities which is commanded by the desire to be worthwhile already make of liberty a dedicated liberty. It is a liberty which realizes itself since the barrier is overcome in which it could still consider itself as a simple power of choice between the eternally rival pretensions of nature and reason. It is such since henceforth it links itself to the history of a desire to be whose soul it is because in it it witnesses to the pure subject.

However, neither cultural goals nor strictly social goals can satisfy the total self. Undoubtedly, they already work at uniting individuals. They create forms of communication based on the identity of norms which preside over action or regulate judgment. They free individual minds from their inner dream by admiration of works in which they can communicate. They work toward awakening individual minds to the sense of their own destiny. Together, however, they do not so much bring minds together as overcome some of the obstacles which separate them. Cultural and social goals only make more acute the experience of the inequality of being with oneself and the need for a deeper communication between minds. The subjects who create these goals understand that they had first to seek themselves through these goals before seeking out one another to reciprocally promote self-consciousness.

However, consciousness can neither be reassured nor even discover that what separates it from itself is identically what separates it from other minds unless it does so through communication. In communication it makes what separates it from another, and the resistance which results unceasingly for the progress of communication, the means of access to self and of verification of the relationship which constitutes it. This indirect advance toward self is the expression of the situation of a consciousness which cannot pretend, without leaving the real conditions of existence, to witness to itself that it has effectively overcome the difference which separates it from its source. Communication cannot free the self from this difference; it can only make this difference more and more self-transparent. Beyond the goals which have begun to deepen the desire to be worthwhile, the proper content of an ethic is the totality of the possibilities of existence which are born for the self from its relations with other minds.

However, there is, first of all, a region of these relations in which minds are in contact only because of what is universal in them and because of their participation in reason. They cannot remain ignorant of this bond without running the risk of a diminution of existence and without gravely compromising the possibilities to be offered to them after the exigencies of reason have been safeguarded in all the breadth of their relationships.

8 / Duty and Existence

IF DUTY, FAITHFULLY OBEYED, does not satisfy our desire to be, at least the self can discover the limits of duty by basing itself on it. Desire must accept the exigencies of duty and extend them if it wishes to preserve from doubt the quality of the aspiration which duty deepens more than it satisfies. Often misunderstanding of the relationships between duty and desire sets off a search for compensations whose costs morality is not alone in bearing. These compensations affect and trouble the aspiration which they sought to defend. The kind of deception which obedience to duty engenders at every instant risks provoking disgust with rules and favoring hypocrisy in moral behavior. The search for pleasure as such is the most unsophisticated form in which the need is manifested to take a kind of revenge against rules and to break the isolation which morality is prompt in realizing when it has only law to unite beings and when, in addition, it separates beings from nature and the world. Even in its most episodic and most disappointing forms, pleasure restores the feeling of an existence which duty cannot contain.

On the fringe of relations governed by reciprocity of duties, communication of another order is initiated in which minds renounce the just pretension defined by moral law, just like two soldiers who, while loyally fighting, suddenly discover in battle that they are linked by a bond stronger, deeper, and more secret than are the reasons which determine their obligation. However, if this communication is destined to grow, the specifically moral order, with its foresight, determination, and universality, must be maintained in the background as a safeguard against the

[115]

misunderstandings or temptations of subjectivity. When relations, dominated by the idea of what is owed or expected, cease, they appear to constitute the grounding without which a higher order remains precarious and ambiguous. When the order of relations is transgressed or ignored—an order whose principle is the recognition of what beings can basically expect universally from one another—all promotion of the communication of minds is compromised.

We must tarry, then, with the disappointment left in the soul by duty, a feeling of disappointment in which we can verify that a certain coincidence of self with self is associated with duty only in rare circumstances. Most often this coincidence is not linked so closely to duty that we have to abstain from comparing our satisfaction with that satisfaction which we experience in other situations accompanied by an authentic growth of being. We do not want to misappropriate the religious significance permeating the expression the self uses when it affirms that it is saved. It characterizes, nevertheless, the certitude of a self restored to possession of its true self, a restoration that happens when we are on a level of existence where it is no longer a question of what minds universally owe to one another in accordance with the moral law. Still, one cannot doubt that, in the ordinary run of life, duty does touch the soul in its center. However, even when there is such cooperation between the self and duty that the self cannot distinguish its being from its duty, nor separate from accomplished duty the irreversible choice which unifies it, this quite perfect adherence does not succeed in hiding the authenticity of the aspiration which moral law can satisfy.

It seems, in fact, that duty has its place in a world in which minds are obliged first of all to obtain an initial success over nature by instituting an order which establishes a zone of protection around each person. Duty asks all to try to modify the motivation of their acts in the same direction. All specifically moral values refer to this order of human relations and to this inner discipline of decisions. Because of this order, minds can address an appeal to one another which issues both from a desire for unity and from a desire for self-transparency which duty manages to awaken but which it cannot satisfy. The possibility of self-accomplishment is offered to the self, not beneath, but beyond duty, or, literally, within duty but not exactly through duty. When the subject of the law does not differ from the subject who, depending on the law, gains possession of himself and can testify that he is, the guarantee which duty gives this experience increases its authority and intensifies its value but does not fundamentally constitute it. What is decisive in this experience is that there is no longer any margin for consciousness between what it does and what it is. Consciousness owes its possibility to be to the relationship which its desire sustains with a primary certitude of which the law is only a symbol. The order of duty contributes to revealing to the self a desire to be whose deepening is identified with ethic itself.

For every individual, his history is the history of this desire, of the radical ignorance of self in which he first finds himself, of the errors into which he allowed himself to be dragged, of the seductions which abused him, and, in the course of the failures which he experienced, of the light finally thrown on his true orientation. No matter how contingent this history is for every consciousness, an ethic must determine its essential moments and thus aid in the enlightenment of the deep will of the individual. The ethic does not prescribe; it reflects on a becoming whose beginning, palpably identical for all, it discerns and whose ideal direction it seeks to discover. If it assigns a goal to this becoming, this is not because it supposes that every consciousness necessarily arrives there. Rather it does this so as not to hide the difficulties encountered by the accomplishment of desire, which infinitely diversify its history. An ethic can only offer itself as the structure of a concrete history which each self begins again and which it does not always complete. The moral imperatives, the order of duty in general, are a moment in this history whose significance it is incumbent upon an ethic to deduce and determine.

One would judge, first of all, that if moral imperatives were indifferent to our desire to be, if they did not correspond in the history of this desire to the moment in which it is a condition of its unfolding that it submit to a law, only with difficulty would one avoid juxtaposing a duty to, or imposing a duty on, a nature which refused it. Even more, if, finally, these moral imperatives did not favor an expansion of this desire, the self would believe that it had discovered a kind of contradiction between duty and an aspiration which one would never persuade it to confuse with a tendency which it might forgo as belonging to a nature deprived of value. This aspiration has nothing in common with the desire for satisfaction related to this or that determined tendency. Nor is it like a synthesis of all tendencies. Whatever help this aspiration might ask of the tendencies, it is not for a goal which would be identical with the goal of any one of them. All tendencies serve this aspiration or are capable of serving it, and no one of them is indispensable to it. They can be lacking to this aspiration even though the satisfaction of which it is capable is not diminished. They can aid this aspiration even though the satisfaction which would witness to its success does not occur.

In order for duty not to be a moment or a condition of the unfolding of our desire to be, it is necessary not only that the diversity of tendencies be unified in themselves but that from their unification a will be spontaneously born. However, a will which would manifest itself through a certain concentration of tendencies would still be only the appearance of a will. The possibility of judging itself by considering itself as two wills would be lacking to this will. Undoubtedly, there is a prefiguration of this judgment in the foresight of which a tendency is capable which has mastered consciousness. There is also a prefiguration of it in the power of this tendency to order a multiplicity of desires to itself. But for all that, this tendency does not escape its own necessity. It would not become true will except by producing in itself a possibility of renunciation. The authority which it exercises only imitates a will. The satisfaction which it engenders deceives the desire to be for which it cannot substitute. Nor can it repress it. The self is as though lost in this willing which is powerless to break away from itself. At this moment there is no chance for an aspiration to directly prevail which can involve itself in a tendency but transcends it as it transcends nature. Only the law is capable of effecting a rupture of this unity instituted by the play of tendencies. At this level the law is the mediation of aspiration into existence because it is equivalent to a negation of spontaneity into which it introduced itself.

Inferring duty is a hazardous enterprise. One can attempt to show, nevertheless, that, if it contradicts the development of instinct, it serves an instinct deeper than all instincts. It is evidence of the action of a desire deeper than all desires. It corresponds to an aspiration deeper than all aspirations born of nature. Reason, which communicates its authority to desire, does not impose itself from on high on a sensibility in rebellion against it but is itself in the service of a desire which no desire of our given being equals. Through duty reason prepares an unfolding of desire which would not otherwise have been possible. The law is the nearest form through which an act is expressed which consciousness is assured is not simply the extension of natural tendencies. It is evidence of a refusal or a suspension of tendencies. Left to themselves in their plurality, or gathered together in a single drive, these tendencies engender a dissatisfaction which cannot help but make consciousness feel that it is on a road which does not lead to itself. Tied to the acquisition of an object which, no sooner attained, slips away, dependent on a world which, when encountered, alternately inflames and disappoints desire, these tendencies dislodge the individual. Hence, since the fundamental desire to be inserts itself invincibly into tendencies and knows itself first of all within them, it reacts to inner dissatisfaction which bothers it by accepting, with the supremacy of a nonempirical act, the authority of a law strong enough to defeat the tendencies. The desire to be withdraws in favor of duty. It is a withdrawal through which it gives itself the chance to find once again, on another level, the same tendencies at its service. Then these tendencies become docile to the realization of an aspiration through which the self enters into possession of itself.

If reason brings in the law, it draws its own power from a desire which uses duty to oppose or suspend the natural movement of tendencies. If one conceives of a reason not secretly sustained by an aspiration of the acting being, its intrusion into life will inevitably appear as constraint. It is better to say that reason itself is desire if one wants to understand the authority it acquires and the way in which it is invited to restore the accord of the soul with itself against the mutual contrariety of tendencies. If it is not directly desire, it is the form which an aspiration, in its relationship to a spontaneity, prisoner of itself and the world, takes on when it seeks to obtain through action and through love an absolute transparency of being to itself.

Once one accepts this aspiration, which is aspiration to unity, it will appear, then, that in a divided world, where each consciousness first of all tends to consider itself the center, moral law and reason arise to symbolize this unity. They prepare its coming or render it eventually easier. The universal which remains relative to many anticipates and substitutes for the concrete modes of any experience of the one. Its condition is that the relations more formally instituted from the point of view of duty and of the universality of the law be transcended. Through duty, although in a manner which empties the desire to be more than it satisfies it, the distance is lessened between the point of departure, at which each man is placed who must begin for himself the history of humanity, and the accomplishment of his being.

For that reason, one will be less astonished that the morality of duty often enunciates its commands in such a way that it becomes impossible to suppose that the self, to which they are addressed and whose expansion they seem to interrupt, nevertheless obeys them as laws which work toward its own desire. Duty masks aspiration. It seems to contradict it only because of the conditions in which it is obliged to unfold itself, that is, in a universe which favors the separation of minds and constrains them to a severe ascesis before they can begin to aim at the unity which they sense in the depths of their desire.

An ethic includes all the moments of what ought to be called the involution of desire if this expression did not risk suggesting that the march toward unity can be consummated and that resistance, which unceasingly conspires to purify and renew desire, can be wiped out. It is a practical involution in the sense that it fulfills itself only through the initiative of consciousness placed in a factual situation which it would seek in vain to infer or to elude. One could not really have a nature, a life, issue from a sovereign affirmation of unity which is at the summit of the movement of reflection. These, nevertheless, are the primordial conditions of this multiplicity and this hostility, spread out in the universe, without which one cannot understand why the place of duty must be so great and its victories so precarious. The nostalgia which duty helps to awaken in the soul is not the memory of lost unity but impatience rising out of obligation when obligation appears to delay the more delicate and deeper movements of love. The principal moments of the history of desire are acts by which consciousness produces itself in instituting an order whose categories are strong enough to block the centrifugal forces which aggravate the inner dissension of tendencies and the opposition of individuals. Duty is one of these moments. It helps aspiration disentangle itself from the knot of natural tendencies. It prepares more substantial satisfactions for aspiration. But in neither its form nor its content can this aspiration be isolated from determinations which it receives from the fact of the givens to which it brings law and rule.

One can discern more exactly this twofold relationship of duty to the essential aspiration of being and to nature by examining from this point of view the function of institutions closely allied to the moral law. While these institutions tend to guarantee a minimum of loyalty between persons, they consolidate the effort of individual minds by creating something like a body in which this effort is conserved. If the institution anticipates the inner fidelity of the subject to the moral law, by furnishing him with a kind of model and by arranging a favorable milieu for him, it completes this fidelity and prolongs it by protecting it against the forgetfulness and weaknesses of willing. Thus the institution becomes something like a nature whose laws both contradict and imitate those of nature. It not only throws up a barrier against the partiality and instability of tendencies in each individual; it interprets these tendencies in the direction of a more intimate willing, which tendencies favor as much as they betray as long as they have not accepted the discipline of a law.

Just like duty, the institution cannot avoid appearing as a constraint if it is not ultimately destined to put the tendencies on which it imposes its rules at the service of the highest aspiration. No institution is lasting which does not concern itself with relating the order which it institutes to desire and to the true will of the individual at the same time that it submits natural inclination to its law. There is a pure inclination which natural inclination blocks as long as the former has not made the latter its surest ally and has not in some manner reabsorbed it. The institution has it as its mission to work there and to require obedience only to promote, beyond the institution, a free accord of pure inclination and natural inclinations in which these latter, far from debasing and impoverishing the former, communicate their strength to it. If the institution fails in this, if it misunderstands the relationship which it has with instincts, or if it takes them into account only to oppose them, it provokes a revenge which the instincts will attempt to exact from it. This happens, as we have seen, to duty.

This characteristic of the institution to be a mediator between nature and liberty allows us to bring back to a common center the problem of the relationship of life to morality and the problem of the relationship of reason to the self and to existence. If one does not distort the idea of life, if one leaves life with all its aggression and competition, it seems it is necessary to choose between two alternatives. Either one opposes morality and life, admitting that they are irreconcilable and thus undoubtedly marking the first with impotency, or, in some way, one sees morality as born from life—but then one does not hide the naturalism to which one rallies. Nevertheless, this choice is far from being so pressing if duty, instead of being an absolute goal, has its condition in existence, which it works to promote. This choice is not so pressing if existence itself is the unfolding of an aspiration which transcends life as such but borrows from tendencies their strength, involves itself in them, and within them produces a conversion of desire. Just as reason, through the universal, is the mediator between primary certitude and the multiplicity of minds, so law and institutions have the function not so much of being opposed to tendencies as of interpreting them in the direction of the aspiration which they must serve and of transmitting them, thus regenerated, to consciousness. The experience of unity of which man is capable beyond the law flows necessarily in the directions designated by the original spontaneity of instincts. A decisive transformation then takes place in the feelings which initially participated in the original vitality. It is a satisfaction which takes nothing away from the depth of their influence in the soul. The function of the institution is to work at this transmutation of tendencies.

The institution succeeds insofar as it orients itself in the direction which would be that of the tendency if this latter could be fully conscious of the finality which it would serve as soon as it gave up posing itself separately and for itself and operated in full agreement with the central aspiration of the self, that is, with a willing which transcends all tendencies and which all tendencies are invited to aid. The first evidence of this aspiration is the need for unity and totality which arises spontaneously out of the diversity of desires. This need is accompanied by a need for continuity, which is a sign of a self seeking to constitute itself despite the intermittent quality of desires and satisfactions. A fundamental contrariety erupts between this finality of unification and concentration and the concurrent and centrifugal finalities of particular tendencies. The institution will fulfill its first function as soon as, relating itself to these tendencies, it interprets them as if each of them had no other goal than to cooperate in the advent of a self capable of will and fidelity. The tendency immediately seeks its own satisfaction, and it does not even have this memory of self which would unify its desires. What it wants even more deeply is not only an integration of self but, beyond its passing desires, a kind of eternity which cannot be assured except through a renunciation by which it moves entirely to another level and consents to allow itself to be absorbed by an aspiration of another order. The institution favors this conversion by setting up a regulation which corresponds to that which a fully self-informed tendency would give itself. As tutor of the tendency, the institution corrects it only to allow it to orient itself freely in the direction of its deepest desire. There are two ways for the institution to misunderstand its function. Either it can limit itself simply to constraining the tendency and to combating it, or it can encourage it and sustain it. These are two contrary errors found in all moral philosophy. One comes from the idea that every natural tendency exercises a disruptive force on institutions; the other comes from the idea that institutions are viable only if they espouse the spontaneous movement of tendencies.

This is a twofold misunderstanding of the power of the institution and of the nature of tendency. If the institution represses, not only must it give up being loved and willed by the being who is subject to it and thus give up promoting morality toward higher forms, but it is unceasingly exposed to the stratagems of the individual. If the institution only reinforces the tendency in its immediacy, it condemns itself to holding all its authority from nature and enters into opposition with the ideal. The consequences are similar; the principles are equally false. What is true for the institution is also true for duty. More generally, the relationship between morality and life is one of neither opposition nor identity; it is, rather, a complex relationship in which institution and rule do not so much constrain nature as free it from itself and reveal to it an aspiration of which at first it was not conscious.

Hegel remarks that, in the absence of a confession on the part of the accused, the jury substitutes itself, one might say, for the consciousness of the accused and interprets his desire in such a way that the punishment can be accepted by him and that he can recognize it as that which he would spontaneously have inflicted on himself. It is an indication of what the sentence might be in every case. This is the most unfavorable, and yet the most significant, example of the relationship between institution and inclination. For the guilty one has not only acted in the past against the law; his will continues to resist confession, and his tendencies are battling the law. It is therefore necessary that the sentence interpret inclination in such a way that, far from being an absolute constraint, it can appear to the subject as the expression of his deep desire and the instrument of his redemption.

The instincts of acquisition, which the institution so often jealously protects when it does not in reaction battle against them, pose no less the problem of the relationship of the institution to inclination. When the institution believes it is doing nothing more than ratifying and consolidating an inclination, one might suspect that this inclination, while not an effect of the institution, is still, under its influence, a contingent determination of an elementary instinct capable of many forms. The institutions of property always oscillate between a position which is for the instinct of acquisition and another which is against it. But in both cases they assume that they have to deal with a tendency that is rigid in its orientation, and they isolate it from a deeper desire of expansion, of which it may be only a narrow and degenerate form. Confident in the plasticity of inclination, the role of the institution here is to lead it, not to radical self-renunciation, but to an understanding of itself as relative to a desire to be for which the appropriation of things must be only a subordinate and secondary means, whose necessity imposes itself only in a world not yet at peace.

It is in an analogous perspective that it is well to consider an institution like marriage in its relation to sexual inclination. If marriage limits itself to regularizing sexual inclination, to maintaining stability of choice against caprice and forgetfulness, it is failing in its more essential function, which is to interpret in the direction of an absolute fidelity the profound wish of the instinct and through this to prepare for the possibility, beyond the guaranteed order of duty and law, of pure relations between minds. This shows better than any other example the character of an institution as a law to which inclination must consent in order to experience itself and to promote itself from within, an inclination which feeds on an aspiration of another order. It is not only the correlation of psychological habit and social habit which is significant in this respect. For both, being effects of the law, threaten to weaken the vigilance of consciousness and to distract it from feeling all that is precarious beneath the appearance of stability in an institution whose true goal would not be a communication of minds freed from all restlessness with respect to duty. It is because it has its goal beyond itself that the institution acquires all its importance at the same time that it seems to render itself useless. The discipline which the institution exercises by aiding in the conversion of an instinct adapts this latter to a higher goal than its immediate goal and mixes it intimately with the most delicate movements of the communication of souls.

Certainly, one must not think that this interpretation of instincts through the institution can be done without meeting resistance. But it must be guided by the idea that such resistance issues as much from nature as from earlier institutions which strengthened them instead of opposing them. It is one and the same thing to think that the reign of duty terminates the unfolding of consciousness and to accept an irremediable break between nature and law. It is true that in its humblest forms human morality emancipates itself from instinct by some regulation which the institution enunciates. But the institution thwarts instinct only to discover better the desire which it covers, which must be brought to self-consciousness. The institution, no less than duty, favors this conversion of instinct. Its chances of success grow in proportion to the attention it brings to limiting the expansion of the natural inclination only with a view to liberating the aspiration whose instrument it is. It seems, then, that in the development of existence the function of duty is relative to a world in which minds, allied to a nature more refractory than agreeable to morality, cannot at first verify the principle which unites them except by opposing instincts and their dissent with the authority of reason and the will of the universal. As the safeguard against both the suggestions of nature and the fantasy of feeling, reason remains for consciousness an irreplaceable guarantee of the value of its inner decisions. As long as the higher forms of union and communication of minds require that always rare conditions of affinity and generosity be fulfilled, as long as the servility of man with respect to nature aggravates the separation of individuals and hides the unity which their desire secretly aims at, the moment of duty, of the institution, of the universal, must substitute for and prepare the most intimate acts of existence.

The greatest responsibility is assumed by consciousness when it decides to give priority over forms of behavior, claiming relationship to the universal and to the law, to a moral inspiration in which the expectation of reciprocity is replaced by gift. At what moment can consciousness no longer expect that institution and duty have sufficiently fortified the rule of law so that there is no longer any need to fear that an aspiration which is like an act of defiance of nature would not on the contrary favor an offensive return of forces hostile to morality? It is a risk whose consequences must be measured. However, the stronger the resistance of the law for an impatient consciousness, the sharper the significance of risk and the less shaky also the advance of morality.

For there to be no possible confusion between the demands of a subjectivity rebellious to every rule and to an authentic progress toward interiority and unity, the link to the universality of duty is no less required than the acceptance of objective tasks. If the satisfactions which supervene upon duty reveal to the self a desire to be whose depth was unknown to it, they are not able to make it forget that they would not have been possible had the self deserted duty. In fact, they have their full intensity only in a universe in which the law has already effected a first revolution with respect to the relation of minds among themselves and to nature. The narrowness of morality when it wishes to recognize only duty comes from this: that it does not know how to perceive in duty itself a necessary step in the history of the tendency to be. It is a tendency which is identified with the history of consciousness, a history verifying and rediscovering at the same time the highest affirmation in a world dedicated to division and to discord, which unceasingly regroup and unceasingly must be limited and combated. Existence is the coming-to-be of this aspiration. No matter what formal characteristic attaches to it because of its correlation to the idea of the universal, duty is nevertheless a moment of a finality which transcends in dignity all empirical finalities.

From this point of view, the problem of the relationships between desire and the good does not present the same difficulties, as long as one distinguishes between the good of finalities assignable to the universe and the good of a finality which can insert itself in one or the other of these finalities but transcends all of them and is not dependent on the possession of any object. What is common to duty and the desire to be is that both are largely independent of all matter and all content and do not have at all the same relationship with the world as tendencies and finalities whose success can be determined. In this, duty already brings us closer to our being. Liberty which acts under the law frees us and, what is even better, gives us access to a liberty which is no longer distinguished from our essence. As long as the desire which constitutes us is identified with empirical tendencies or is so close to them that it is not able to distinguish itself from them, it expects from the world satisfactions which will soon disappoint it. It follows from this that liberty defines itself as a power capable of wresting itself free of the solicitations of inclination. It also follows that liberty allies itself with duty and sets up an opposition between duty and the good. But duty throws light on and restores for itself an aspiration which inclinations masked. Our intimate willing is then liberty, and liberty coincides with essence. Its good is beyond all goods envisaged by finalities solidary with nature and the world.

From an analogous point of view, an ethic of responsibility is prompt to direct itself toward a compromise less mindful of fidelity to ideas than attentive to the consequences of action in a world in which, unless one is imprudent, one cannot ignore the disorder of passions or the instability of wills. On the other hand, the ethic of love or of faith is too complaisant when the feeling from which it flows, becoming indifferent to the concrete conditions of its efficacy, acts in the manner of a principle blind to the effects which lead tasks undertaken to ruin. The unreality of this ethic condemns it, just as its realism discredited the ethic of responsibility, whose principle was just, as long as it consisted in the refusal to take into account the rivalry of beliefs and the structure of the milieu of action. It is when they have already degenerated that these two ethics are opposed to one another and appear to be irreconcilable. This degeneration happens even more rapidly for an ethic of love since it presents itself in the form of precepts or of formulas of action instead of only affirming itself as a secret aspiration of feeling. For as soon as facts give the lie to it and constrain it to decline, this ethic of love can maintain itself only by increasing its intransigence or by accept-

ing a kind of status which profoundly alters its original signification. The decadence of an ethic of responsibility inclines toward
an opportunism defiant in the face of every principle once the
preoccupation with consequences alone wins out over the firm
decision to mold the real to the exigencies of the ideal.

Certainly there is no question of denying the diversity of
moral vocations. However, just as the opposition between an
ethic of intention and an ethic of consequences is sharp when it
is detached from existence and formulated abstractly, so this
opposition begins to be attenuated when it is related to the
different moments of the expansion of desire. No moral theory
of intention will require one to consider indifferently the content
of decision if it remains attentive to the relationship between
subjectivity and world. It is the unconditionality at the heart of
aspiration which creates an apparent divorce between an ethic
determined to avow only actions capable of giving satisfaction to
the desire to be and an ethic anxious to retain among its givens
the totality of conditions which arouses the division of minds,
calls forth an order of their relations founded on an exact reciprocity, and maintains at the center of these relations the presence of a nature avaricious of its aid. No serious debate takes
place in a soul without consciousness asking itself if it ought not
forgo its concern for reciprocity modeled on its certitude and its
desire for unity. But what is this impatience worth if consciousness forgets that its hunger for the absolute can first of all find
sustenance in the order of duty? Rather than be a sacrifice, its
act could be an evasion. When the aid of law is lacking to the
higher forms of existence, they are exposed to being marked
with a character of insincerity and unreality.

Is it only an aid? There is no disobedience of the law which
does not experience itself in terms of the law and does not
conceive itself in its singularity as capable of law. There is no act
of pardon or renunciation of the command of justice which can
isolate itself from the command of justice and which does not
maintain the idea at the very moment it seems to be contradicting it. Further, there is no submission to the law which must not
welcome within itself the thought of a splendor of action superior to the law, nor a will to justice which can ratify itself if it is
not transfused by the desire to love. The somber side of existence
persists even in the pure forms of self-disinterestedness, and the
danger of confusion always remains for consciousness between

a renunciation out of weakness and a renunciation which is evidence of more strength than defense of right would demand. That is what one must ask of prophets of love and what one must remind them of. The approach of the most delicate and the deepest moments of love is accompanied by a refinement, not by a suppression, of acts which reserve to each consciousness its own sphere. Strength cannot be absent from the very act which renounces the use of strength. The obscuring of the generative principle of value makes this desire to be retain in its own depths this duality and this relationship.

Bitterness would not be mixed with satisfaction if the determination of duty did not often imply a renunciation of the highest values. But duties are not hierarchized, as values are, and the tension which results from this relationship is rarely absent from choice. This is why there is joined, to the *élan* which incites us no longer to spare our will, the feeling of more elementary values, without which every sacrifice would risk being in vain. If decision had to regulate itself according to the hierarchy of values, fault would begin at the moment in which the choice of duty did not correspond to the highest value. Inversely, consciousness would feel itself exempt from all fault when this correspondence existed. Who would believe that moral experience is that simple?

If, in many circumstances, duty requires one to give up, at least for a time, activities which look directly to the fulfillment of consciousness in a peaceful world, it is because the bases of morality are still far below what the self would require in order to dare to give itself fully and without regret to purposes of another order. In a manner of speaking, duty suspends all activities not subject to practical reason as long as practical reason has not yet obtained the most elementary satisfactions. With respect to our fundamental aspiration, society, in the form in which it has issued from nature, offers itself as both what is most desirable and most hostile: what is most desirable, because nothing will respond as much to the secret will of existence as a reign capable at all levels of promoting the communication of minds; what is most hostile, because in it the separation of beings finds itself at every instant aggravated and becomes a scandal because of the complicities of consciousness and instinct. Whereas everywhere else nature presents itself without a mask, for man it is no longer so. This is why the social bond is such that it must be at the same time loosened and tightened: loosened because it is oppressive and constraining; tightened because it is naturally too loose to stop natural inclination from seeking its revenge against the discipline to which it is subject. Thus the reign of the social, which cannot conceivably be neglected by the movement which awakens consciousness to itself, also opposes the greatest resistance to an aspiration which transcends the social as such. The compensations which this aspiration seeks in purposes removed from the domain of the social only make more intolerable the disavowal which the social inflicts on this aspiration. While these compensations orient consciousness in a direction which distracts it at first from working for the transformation of the social bond, it happens that this social bond appears to be more and more exterior to the aspiration of being. Thus, practical reason, whose function consists in interpreting this aspiration and in removing resistance which gets in its way, can fulfill its function only through rules. The effect of these rules is to hide the aspiration from itself. Instead of understanding these rules in their relationship to pure inclination, which they must guide and free, the individual understands them only in their relationship to natural tendencies which they contain or repress. From this follows that very apparent character which life takes on of being obedient to imperatives which, in order to restore the primacy of the social, require the individual not to accede to the suggestion of the instincts. At this moment, every connection seems broken between the true desire of the self and the prescriptions of morality, as well as between these latter and the other purposes in which consciousness seeks to obtain satisfaction for its repressed aspiration. The self allowed itself to be divided. In vain does it seek to unify itself by absolute dedication to a purpose of its own choice; in vain would it like to find there the equivalent of all virtues. The arrest suffered by the promotion of values in social life becomes a factor of delay which universally affects desire.

Thereupon, the speculative or aesthetic activities seem suddenly devalued and no longer seem to merit the resources of the individual. Must one abandon to itself the history of societies as if it were subject to a natural, invincible fatality and in the name of a transcendent optimism consider indifferent to the salvation of the soul the destiny of man as a part of the social whole to which we belong? Do we think we might re-establish a broken equilibrium for morality through individual asceticism? Or would we want to compensate for this loss of *élan*, this arrest of morality within given societies, with societies issuing from free creation? Should we consider the political order as radically contingent upon the development of the objective spirit? Each of these answers constitutes for the will to existence the admission of failure. Consciousness cannot give up, without harming itself, the work of instituting an order without which the changes of the interior life would be only a game. In order for the tragic to unfold itself in depth at all levels of existence not touched by the political and social order, satisfaction must have been given to duty. Certainly, duty works toward its own suppression. But the conditions from which it deduces itself are always remade, only more subtly. The attraction of sacrifice is that of an act which would give us access to a world in which the absolute exigency which is at the foundation of our desire would no longer have to remember duty.

The value accorded to intention betrays the nostalgia of a desire forced to substitute, for a good which would satisfy it, a satisfaction drawn from consciousness alone of the inner direction of willing and charged with compensating for the disappointment of an effort in the world, where moral success is ambiguous and uncertain. Duty cannot command without at once inciting consciousness not to expect, in order to assure itself of the absolute quality of its willing, that there be some proportion between its effort and the success of purposes to which it applies itself. What is stranger than this refusal to judge our willing on its real benefaction, on its real consequences for other minds? Neither the archer who aims at a target nor the pilot of a boat judges himself on his intentions, at least as long as his judgment is that of an archer or a pilot. Is what is proper to morality, in opposition to all technical activities, that it can remain indifferent to its efficiency and withdraw into itself? But there is a matter of duty which is not to be identified with the matter of utilitarian purposes. Undoubtedly. But what is this matter? The good of other persons. What good? That they possess the truth which I know, that they receive the riches which are due to them and the esteem to which they have a right? Undoubtedly. But how avoid at once admitting that the determination of this matter is relative to a world in which minds do not so much work to promote reciprocally their profound aspiration as to remove first of all the obstacles whose presence paralyzes the *élan* which would carry them beyond duty? The value of intention is deduced from it, along with the kind of agnosticism to which it is allied. This value can only decrease as duty withdraws. This is the case with every ontological optimism in which there is consonance between willing and being.

One might presume that this is what also happens in philosophies in which so-called material values, accessible to intuition, are the object of a preference of which it would be contradictory to think that it attributes to its own act a value capable of counterbalancing or of equaling the value of these values. On the contrary, these doctrines are led to restore to intention a value which without difficulty surpasses that of properly designated values which constitute the matter of morality. This most significant trait is related not only to the "sporadic" character of the intuition of values and to their heterogeneity but to the necessity of depending on the acting subject and on his liberty to return its unity and its specificity to the moral life. If the value of intention does not entail the "material" values which the subject envisions, it nevertheless concentrates in itself morality properly speaking, which does not depend on the real success of action or on the realization of its content. The will renounces the ambition of a response to its act. Through intention consciousness reassures itself as to the possible failure of its action, and from this bias duty, which one thought one could dispense with, reassumes a central place in concrete morality.

Nothing is richer in meaning for understanding the relationship between duty and existence than this disavowal inflicted on themselves by doctrines whose center of gravity seemed at first to be sought for in an adequation of consciousness and content but now is related to intention. Is this not the sign that, in any ontology where morality is not identified with the assimilation of will to being, duty and intentional willing manifest the delay which this assimilation suffers? One wanted to give them no more than a completely subordinate place; but, as the route to be traveled is lengthened, one puts them in the first place. The declared primacy of intention in other doctrines confirms the same thesis. They do not succeed in hiding the fact that the value of intention, far from being absolute, is in inverse ratio to the hope which we place in the efficacy of our action in the promotion of morality.

The initial depreciation of intention, as well as the frank recognition of its value, draws its significance only from the correct relationship of duty to existence. It does not answer the difficulty to abandon to duty a domain which one acknowledges does not touch upon the deep interests of consciousness. Duty takes vengeance by suddenly bringing itself to the attention of the individual in situations which leave him no choice but to act out of duty or to fail his inner being. However, it is also useless to deny that consciousness seeks beyond duty for more substantial satisfactions. Neither duty nor the responsible acts which accompany it would have the power to defeat the natural inclinations of the individual if the inclinations in ignorance of self did not serve an aspiration in which a radical certitude of duty is expressed. To betray duty is to betray this aspiration; to fulfill duty is to recognize at once that it is only the promise and the condition of an order in which existence will be reconciled with itself.

Nothing better illustrates or verifies this conclusion than what are commonly called the conflicts of duty. While the highest interest of the self is not to allow itself to be divided, the rivalry of duties which tears consciousness asunder manifests sharply what is already implied in the simplest relationship between duty and existence. A more subtle and a more moving perception of this relationship, the feeling that this relationship opens up on another horizon—this is the new experience which the self has. Whether it is a question of the intrinsic opposition of duties or only of contingent noncompossibility in a given situation, the effort of the subject to restore its unity by creative decision alerts it to a meaning of obligation which the apparent harmony of duty and self hid from it. This harmony was obtained at the price of some abdication whose importance consciousness learns of only because of conflict. It was necessary for the self, withdrawing into its duty, to agree to ignore the link of this duty to a world still bent on division and struggle and to refuse to hear the appeal of an aspiration which would have troubled its tranquillity.

The conflict reveals to the self a desire and possibilities of existence which duty had previously worked to repress. Provoked by the conflict, the rupture of the accord between duty and the self brings to light discord between the self and its being or, at least, an inequality which is linked to the permanent conditions in which moral effort is accomplished. Consciousness is surprised by the conflict to the extent that, up to that moment, it had been indifferent to all limitation, partiality, and, sometimes, blind preferences involved in morality. It seems that it stuck more closely to duty the more it was insensible both to the truth of its desire and to antagonisms, to the separation of beings and to the misery of the environing morality. If duty is often the form which is taken on by a determination of morality related to a division of groups, to latent hostilities, to traditional jealousies, worried about every change; if duty is often the mask which is donned by an attachment to rules and to discipline which constrains tendencies only to do more violence to the aspiration for which that could be the instrument; if obedience and fidelity to the law sometimes do not escape being self-complacency and pharisaism, one can see that the apperception of a conflict and the test to which it submits a consciousness are a crisis capable at one and the same time of promoting morality and of bringing the self closer to its being. In this crisis the relationship of duty to existence is sufficiently deepened that the self can no longer doubt, if it has not suppressed by its creative action the conditions for which, unceasingly, new conflicts will be born, that it has won a growth of its being by becoming conscious of an aspiration which forbids it henceforth both to refuse duty and to take refuge in it.

Likewise, at the same time that its aspiration tends toward an appropriation of the highest affirmation, the conflicts of duties alert consciousness to the fact that it has by no means exhausted the ground in which its will is rooted. Nothing is more frequent than neglect of elementary values when consciousness is concerned only for the rarest and most delicate values. Not that its wish is to do harm or to injure these elementary values. But, in the movement which carries it along, consciousness does not generally think of assuring itself of a simultaneous promotion of all values. Nor does consciousness take care that the conditions be safeguarded without which the success of value is so fragile that it risks, subsequently, either appearing to be inaccessible or requiring a radical renunciation of all that in this world is capable of conservation and growth. There can be no doubt as to the constant and most general consequences of a vision of the highest values when this vision is not accompanied or preceded by a discipline safeguarding the most solid values. If this vision does not include in the consciousness of the individual, or even in the will of a group, the acceptance of the risk of death; if death does not appear as the foreseeable penalty for radical devotion of the being to these values; if, inversely, this vision is accompanied by negligence and indifference for all that which one can consider as the foundations of morality in the subject, consequences are soon felt. It is no longer anything but a sick will which has charge of values, for which, on the contrary, the most delicate and persevering attention is required. Disaffection and doubt soon touch values toward which the hope of consciousness was drawn. These values become depreciated to the extent that the envisioning of them seems responsible for the weaknesses produced at the level of elementary morality.

It becomes more and more difficult to decide whether it is the will which has betrayed the ideas which it should serve or whether it is the ideas which must be denounced. There is nothing surprising, then, if certain situations which generate conflicts are the expression of the deeper opposition between a morality whose ideal remains intransigent and the need to be mindful of the most elementary values nearer to the possibilities of nature. The general decline of morality which the affirmation of the superiority of higher values can entail, when it is not at all sustained by the effective appropriation of values of a lower rank, is a fact whose interpretation is linked to the obfuscation of the generative principle of value. The greater and greater oscillations of moral and political movements, the crises which affect Western life, belong to the same problem. Beneath the rhythm which they present, one has no difficulty in seeing the decline of ideas which inspire a democratic and socialist conception of institutions or which aim at transporting into social relations a religious inspiration. This decline brings back a conception of the social and human order which, if not naturalistic, is at least severe and defiant with respect to all the pretensions of consciousness to establish an order which contradicts that order for which the givens of social and individual human nature furnish the conditions and rigorously limit the development. Curiously wedded in well-known thinkers who profess philosophical spiritualism are a speculative idealism and a profound pessimism concerning the chances of managing to manifest here below even a reflection of the supernatural. The otherworldliness which accompanies this spiritualism, as far as the efficacy of moral ideas in nature and society is concerned, seems to support the strictest sort of positivism in the human order, which is viewed in such a way that hope for concrete progress in social morality is derided by both realism and speculative spiritualism. On this point, the contemporary philosopher who is most heeded compensates for the mysticism of morality and religion by an analysis of human nature whose conclusions badly damage the too easy and always disappointed hopes of a reform of potential instincts or of the elementary structures of morality and human societies. Because it corresponds to a true victory over a cosmic fact, the conversion of man to morality involves in his estimation a radical break with nature. To erase the secular bent of habits, nothing less is necessary than an operation capable of annulling an organic necessity contemporary with creation. Such a victory can only be rare. Far from seeking collaboration with transcended nature, morality rather fears the fall which is the law of all life. Thus everything happens as if each of these exceptional victories, having in fact to give up maintaining itself as such or spreading its example, rather served to accentuate the fatality which fixes the level and the conditions of morality for individuals and for societies.

All these reasons and other analogous evident reasons contrive to favor the thought of a necessary option between an idealism attentive to the most delicate values but impotent and a morality concerned above all with the most urgent values, those which are closest to those which require the least sacrifice of nature and even limit themselves to espousing the directions of our instincts. Undoubtedly, sometimes one conceives something like a zone of aspirations radically foreign to the wishes of nature reacting against an elementary morality, provoking in it a certain uplift and joining with it to form notions drawing their authority from forces coming from below and from values which issue from the most generous movements of the human soul. But this mixture does not so much appease the conflict as aggravate it. It puts at the service of instinct ideas which, directed away from their original inspiration, are bent in the direction of nature. It is true that it could not be otherwise if these ideas take root in ground which has not yet prepared a certain culture of

feelings and a will for receiving them. Then they exhaust very
rapidly the individuals or the groups who take it upon themselves to defend them. The ideas themselves come out of this
experience quite exhausted. The weakness of wills which should
have appropriated them becomes their own weakness. They fall
into discredit, and their appearance in the world of phenomena
corresponds to a loss of value.

After the self, menaced by oppositions, has attempted
through its choice to reformulate its unity, the bitterness which
mixes with satisfaction shows sufficiently that the relationship
of duty to existence is never exempt from a tension in which are
found again, transported to a more subtle matter, the givens
with which duty is allied. The possibles which the self renounced, the imperatives for which it perhaps proffered an appeal which places it closer to its being, if they do not succeed at
all in delaying the ascending movement of self-consciousness, if
on the contrary they strengthen it by their resistance, nevertheless let their presence be felt. It is not certain that in the exaltation of sacrifice there is not still, to wound consciousness, the
memory of the rivalry of values in which duty reaffirms and
intensifies itself.

From another point of view, better than duty, from which all
hesitation is absent, can do it, choice, which resolves this rivalry
of values with an exact idea of the commerce of minds and of
reason, prohibits all confusion between the expansion of existence and the defense of individuality as such. The failure inflicted on a logic of morality which knows only the subsumption
of a single decision under a universal law transforms, without
abolishing it, the relationship between consciousness and reason. As long as the self can judge its actions only from the single
point of view of their accord or their disaccord with the law, it
must fear that an aspiration different from reason will pass for
the expression of the individual and his instincts. If the subject
of duty is the rational subject, resistance to the law issues, it is
thought, from the individual who is below the law; the irrational
comes entirely from this side. But as soon as the logic of subsumption is succeeded by the movement of a consciousness
invited to discover its duty, that is, to choose the level of existence at which it wants to place itself, what is unique and irreducible in its act, the originality which it manifests, does not
contradict the law, but, quite to the contrary, pays homage to it.

The opposition between an empirical or sensible self, more or less constrained by the law, and a pure, rational consciousness gives way to a relationship between a concrete self and reason in which reason, prepared by an aspiration which transcends it, in its lucidity and its disinterestedness serves the true interests of liberty. Thus it could be that, in assuming against the law the responsibility of a deeper fidelity to the law, consciousness might nevertheless be assured of betraying neither the highest affirmation nor reason.

What support the deep life of consciousness can expect from reason is misunderstood as long as it is considered evident that all that is not reason belongs to psychological subjectivity as such, as long as, on the other hand, one expects from a depreciation of reason the triumph of an order of belief or of the heart. Nevertheless, nothing can be more favorable to an enlargement of the role of reason than the discovery of a subjectivity freed from the tutelage of the intelligible world but so much the more attentive to avoiding confusion with the purely psychological or with an emotional life which one can always suspect of reflecting the hidden play of instinct. A line of demarcation can be traced by reason between a causality condemned to remain noncommunicable and a causality capable of illuminating and judging itself without breaking its ties to the self. Because it was feared that reason was indifferent or hostile to the intimateness of being and that it did not favor an entirely objective conception of man, it was thought that the time of universalism had been rolled back. An existentialism promptly emptied of all that is truly existential seemed to lend its aid to a subjectivity cut off from reason. It was not seen that a disarmed reason would no longer allow one to recognize the advance of existence through the mediation of duty.

9 / Experience of the One
in the Interchange of Minds

THE PROMOTION OF MORALITY through duty creates the conditions of possibility for a communication of minds. It gives the desire to be deeper satisfaction in an experience in which the relationship of existence to its source, carried to another level, is rediscovered. Just as duty is not so much opposed to inclinations as it interprets them, to bring them into agreement with the inner aspiration of the acting being, so communication, animated by this aspiration and sustained by a will to veracity, does not have to create from scratch the relationships and the structures of the exchanges in which it is accomplished. Communication has only to gather together the forms of spontaneous communication of minds in order to make them serve its design, that is, serve the promotion of existence. This communication of minds does not suppose as given before its act, each with the feeling of its own subjectivity, the minds in which it must, on the contrary, engender self-certitude. At every level, communication relies on consciousness of self which a more basic communication has produced. At no time is a consciousness capable of growth in being without being initially beholden to its dialogue with another consciousness.

However, this whole question is obscured by the hold which object categories exercise in an area where their authority should cease. The distinction between an I which plays the invariant role and a self which, thanks to the I, thinks about and judges itself, far from being of the same order as the relationship of subject to object, can be constituted only by the interruption of a dialogue which minds carry on without, in the beginning,

[139]

having a clear sense of a for-itself. Consciousness, addressing itself by taking the form of an I, assumes the function which
another consciousness fulfilled. The intermittence of exchange
creates a kind of vacuum and leaves disappointment, which
seeks compensation in this relation of the I and the self in which
the I questions, counsels, and reprimands the self as did another
self in spontaneous communication. The being which is sum-
moned to respond to another consciousness guards the memory
of this appeal and maintains its conditions when it engages in
dialogue with itself.

Transcendent categories, which tend to represent a multiplicity of persons destined to enter into interchange with one
another by the breaking up of a supraconsciousness, also falsify
the understanding of the communication of minds because they
are already ontologically allied through their common deriva-
tion. It is very clear that in this way one still endorses forms of
exteriority according to which one conceives that relations between given beings are determined. There is no common measure, there is no analogy of any kind, between these relationships
and the acts which for minds arouse self-knowledge and a radical promotion of their being. No less serious is the error of
rooting exchanges between minds in a pre-existing concrete totality. Right away these exchanges fall to the level of secondary
and conditioned processes whose temporal nature does not succeed in guaranteeing a fundamental and authentic teleological
character.

The welcome given one consciousness by another consciousness does not involve any judgment of an earlier reality. It is the
experience of a presence; this moment is an act whose spontaneous or premeditated modalities correspond to spontaneous or
premeditated modalities of an appeal. Welcome and appeal en-
rich each other, develop and deepen in an experience whose
allied moments they are, in a reciprocity which must not be
compared with that conceived according to forms of theoretical
thought. A consciousness nourished by this reciprocity cannot
think itself nor pose itself for itself as a subject capable at will of
abstracting itself from this relation or of offering itself to it. The
appeals heard and the replies which send out new appeals constitute a single experience, in which acts are interdependent in
such a way that no one of them accedes to its own causality or to
its own interiority except through the other to which it responds

or whose response it detects. Each of the forms in which consciousness of self is produced in withdrawal is correlative of a group of acts which have meaning only through one another and one for another before taking their origin in two distinct poles.

If, after consciousness has constituted the idea of a self, it interrogates itself about the way to restore communication, it creates a problem which must seem insoluble to it. How relate separated minds if each is for itself and unto itself its whole world? Having contrived to create the feeling of interiority, communication has made itself incomprehensible to itself. A new communication dispels the mystery and, since it gives rise to a subjectivity richer than the first, it recreates this subjectivity at the same time on another level. There is no friendship or love undisturbed by the experience of this separation, which does not, nevertheless, become for each consciousness the condition for deepening of self.

Thus the self constructs the idea that there is a secret of the inner life, which it is free to hide or to unveil at will. The possibilities of existence constituted around these acts—silence, confession, and lie—are a decisive moment in the history of consciousness of self. Born of communication, these possibilities soon appear to exist prior to communication. An ethic then becomes the relationship of these possibilities to the act of consciousness which opts for one of them. From this moment on, it is true that a consciousness' experience of being is constructed out of its opposition to excluded possibilities as well as out of their resistance. Neither love nor confidence nor truthfulness could have become a positive value if the contrary possibilities had not been sketched out as subjectivity was born from communication.

These positive values are the different modes of a desire for unity which communication reveals to itself. However, communication both disappoints and inflames this desire, at one and the same time, by occasioning the experience of separation, aggravated by representation of a distinct plurality, as soon as it suffers the intrusion of forms of exteriority. Negative values, which are the values of withdrawal, are allied to this experience of the separation of minds, contemporaneous with the birth of subjectivity and the for-itself. Thus, the original acts of communication, by a kind of splitting, polarize into centers which create the idea of their independence. The contrary possibilities of expansion and isolation are born out of this. A consciousness is defined by them when they would not have been born if communication in the living unity of questions and answers had not allowed the self to have access to self.

The most intimate aspiration of the being is expressed by nostalgia for this unity. But once this unity has been broken, after the feeling of for-itself has developed in each consciousness, after new exchanges and new attempts through multiple trials and errors have fortified in the self belief in an entirely inner world which is its own, acts of communication can no longer have the character they once had. They are now accompanied by expectations, reservations, and intentions which adapt them to the supposed intentions of another consciousness. For the original correlation of intentions which were born spontaneously in communication there is substituted a subtle game in which sometimes in each partner there is present the thought of fooling the other. Prudence is joined to acts, and the repression and command of one's emotions which accompany these acts add a new note to the feeling of for-itself. Friend and enemy are determined by the quality and correspondence of acts and by the experience of their successes or failures.

Nevertheless, beneath these intentions, withdrawing one from another, there persists the memory of the unity of the operation beginning with which minds, each returning to itself, proceeded toward the conquest of their own inner life. The idea of this unity is present in acts which seem only to aim at the deepening of subjectivity. In the dialogue of the self with itself this unity remains efficacious, as if this dialogue were only a preparation for the moment when communication would restore a more assured unity. When it seeks deeper communication, consciousness is sustained by the memory of these original experiences. These experiences instructed consciousness about the kind of acts of which it is capable. They traced the figure of a being capable of promise, capable of confession or pardon. They created, because of the deepening of the interiority which prolonged them, possibilities of existence which now offer themselves to the option of consciousness. Never has an appeal been heard, never has a prayer been answered, never has a confession been heard without its being at the origin of a new idea of our being. Reason itself, in its universal requirement of reciprocity, defines itself for itself only within the agreement of human minds in which it first of all acquired the feeling of its power. There would be less reason to fear that the prestige of reason might diminish the more concrete forms of communication if one saw reason being constituted within communication.

The hesitation which we experience with respect to our being is therefore a hesitation between possibilities of existence pre-formed in the spontaneous communication of minds. However, at what moment do these possibilities obtain for the self a value which affects it in its innermost being and seem to it proper for promoting its existence at a level which is not that of duty? It is when, within the intermittencies of a communication, freed from purposes whose instrument at first it is, and attentive to itself and capable of solitude, the self discovers that the dialogue in which it is engaged with itself not only in its form and in its content draws all its substance from communication but is destined to deceive a desire to be which could flourish if only communication, enriched with an interiority it made possible, had no other goal than to serve this purpose without end which is the reciprocal recognition of minds and the exaltation of their being.

However, nothing determines a consciousness to accomplish the absolute act by which it affirms the subjectivity of another consciousness and makes of this affirmation the condition of communication in which it is ready to welcome into itself, as coming from another absolute initiative, responses, appeals, and confessions. If spontaneous communication, servant of natural tendencies and finalities, gathers together the most favorable conditions for this act, it does not exclude a contrary act by which consciousness decides to annul within itself the being and the truth of other minds. The most decisive moment for the history of a consciousness is assuredly that in which it discovers that its most secret and most free act opens up for it the hope of a liberty which, because of the growth in being which accompanies it, infinitely transcends in value the initiative which made it possible. At the same time that consciousness radically re-nounces the illusion of being all being for itself, it conquers, it receives in exchange, the possibility of existing for other minds. It begins a communication which cannot take on depth without producing an advance in existence.

This free conversion to the affirmation of other minds peoples the world with existences which constitute a universe always menaced with dissolution by the possibility of treason or perjury. But it does not happen in such a way that afterwards everything transpires as though nothing had changed. It is not possible for this reciprocal recognition of minds to be broken without profoundly affecting the modes of communication which follow upon it. While the limitations or the failures of spontaneous communication were due to repugnancies, to lack of understanding, and to accidents, the will to ignore or to refuse the existence of other minds, from which we received growth in our being, gives a new meaning to hate, hostility, and all the modes of divided existence. The negative values of withdrawal and opposition are determined and accentuated as a function of the positive values of love. The bond which united minds makes its presence felt in their separation. Intentions immanent in inimical acts remain allied to those which at first effected agreement of minds. From original communication which precedes consciousness of self to reciprocal affirmation of minds, and from this latter to a subjectivity which wants to withdraw into itself, the unifying unity changes nature and value but by no means disappears. The most decided antagonisms would die out of themselves if the adversaries, whether they wanted to or not, whether they knew it or not, did not remain united by a bond more solid than their hate.

How should we understand this unity? Does not this conversion to the affirmation of other minds usurp the role which only a universal consciousness could play? When an individual consciousness believes that by its own means it recognizes the existence of another consciousness, does it do anything other than recognize the universal consciousness on which all minds depend for their being? Would not minds remain invincibly separated without this bond of universal consciousness, the mediator of all affirmations and of all communication? Does not the initiative by which a consciousness welcomes into itself, as coming from a particular subjectivity, an appeal which it hears imply an antecedent unity without which it would remain illusory and deprived of all fecundity for the communication which should follow from it? If to sustain the communication of minds there is no experience which each consciousness has of its relationship to an absolute consciousness, what can be the guarantee for the act which begins communication between two individual minds? Undoubtedly, this antecedent and always enveloping experience relegates to a secondary role the act in which we thought we saw a decisive moment for the promotion of existence. However, while losing first importance, does not this act regain self-assurance and a foundation which it lacked?

One goes to the heart of the problem if one poses it in its relationship to the experience of an absolute presence—an experience of which no individual communication can be jealous because it is in virtue of it that the individual communication understands itself. This experience is a unique relationship, not subject to the conditions under which the communication of individual minds begins and develops; it is an incomparable reciprocity, such that, neither of the minds having to fear the obstacle of refusal of audience, each is assured of receiving infinitely more than it can give by its own act; it is an interchange whose actuality, incapable of ever being broken, suffers apparent interruption from only one side by the interruption of attention or of prayer; it is a certitude whose influence is mutual but in which neither of the minds affects or creates the history of the other in a manner in which it is itself affected and regenerated; it is feelings of humility corresponding to an inexhaustible manifestation of love. All these characteristics of the experience of absolute presence overshadow a communication bound to producing and maintaining itself under conditions which give the lie to, and always contradict, the certitude of unity but which raise so much the more the price of a victory of friendship or of love.

Does not the experience of an absolute presence relegate communication of minds to a secondary level? Does it not introduce into this communication a limitation which it must despair of overcoming? When it yields to the enjoyment of communication, does not a consciousness tend to forget that the being of the other consciousness maintains with absolute consciousness a relationship which it must forgo penetrating? It is a relationship which adds to the original differences between two minds an absolute difference which their reciprocal gifts cannot reduce or attentuate and which never ceases to menace the mutual advance and creation of existence which each mind wants itself to be capable of. Since its relationship to an absolute consciousness cannot but enter into the constitution of the inner being of each consciousness, the communication of individual minds for this reason finds itself affected by the history and crises of an essential communication other than its own, whose secret entirely escapes it.

One might venture to say that in this instance it is evident that only experience should be opposed to experience. However, the danger of making final statements warns one off. When the experience of an absolute presence is lacking, it is true that the desire for reciprocity never has the assurance of having been fulfilled. This desire for reciprocity cannot hope for absolute satisfaction in the communication of minds. But it is accompanied by a certitude of unity which, in becoming immanent in the generative intentions of communication, cannot be defeated by the ruptures or the failures of the bond of reciprocity.

While the experience of an absolute presence leaves communication with only a subordinate role, consciousness, which has lifted itself for itself to the intuition and affirmation of unity, requires of communication the accomplishment of its certitude on the terrain of history. In history communication becomes truly creative. Whether consciousness attains concentration and regeneration by return to the highest certitude or unfolds itself in communication which satisfies its most intimate desire, this rhythm must not hide the solidarity of the two moments. Communication translates into becoming and into effort what relationship to the highest certitude affirms in the timelessness of its act. Everything issues from the primacy of a unitive experience through which each consciousness understands, subsequently, in the idea of self both the being it owes to the act of the other as well as the act by which it gives being to another. What the other consciousness is in me in communication, the being which it acquires through me and, reciprocally, the transformation of my own being by the act of the other consciousness—all issue from this unitive experience. The twofold movement, the exchange by which I make the other consciousness exist in me while it makes me exist in it, and the promotion of being which results for both, also issue from this unitive experience.

The possibility of an absence of reciprocity only enhances the significance of this experience, for the highest certitude in which the communication is rooted is not the certitude of reciprocity but affirmation of unity, which does not exempt minds from a free conversion to love or protect them against the return of solitude. Nevertheless, beneath refusal, beneath resistance, beneath hostility itself there hides a secret hesitation between love and hate, an oscillation between the one and the other in which there remains, along with the possibility of self-giving, the memory of a unitive experience without which there would not have been formulated at the same time as consciousness of self the act of refusal or negation of the other.

From this point of view it seems clearer that the highest certitude is like a summit through which reflection passes and to which it can always return, not to lose itself or to renounce itself, as do individual minds in the realism of the One, but to return immediately toward unitive experiences whose progress it conditions. The *élan* toward the One would be a sterile *élan* if it were not wholly transmuted into the desire to have the communication of minds serve the promotion of existence. Consciousness could wish to contain itself within the affirmation of unity only if it forgot itself as a being to which appeals are directed and to which responses come. If the inner act by which the self regrasped the highest certitude did not conspire with unitive experiences, the world would be fated to division. Consciousness of self, which is the fruit of communication, knows the weakening of its being because of the authority which numerical categories exercise over it in a disjointed universe in which minds seeing themselves as many seek vainly to reconstitute a whole. Deprived of the help of the highest affirmation, unitive experiences, after having made consciousness of self possible, will never succeed in opposing the representation of a distinct plurality of minds constituting so many worlds closed to one another.

This representation, which in the final analysis consists in an objectification of subjects, is itself the expression of conditions to which our unitive experiences are allied, but at first they are unaware that this is so. These are conditions which do not originally imply numerical categories or objective space or time but which adapt to these categories by denaturing themselves as soon as the representation undertakes to explain for itself the possibility of communication between separated beings. What was originally opacity of consciousness, resistance to unitive experience, bond with natural tendencies and desires, utilization of material means and of one's own body for communication becomes, in the language of categories, plurality of distinct centers, to each of which an independent subjective life seems to be attached. Categories of the object come in a way to the rescue of emotions of withdrawal or defense to make communication more difficult.

In this respect, even though it is only fictitious, the idea of a pure monadology at the level of ontology can serve to throw light by way of opposition on the character of our unitive experiences. By pure monadology we should understand a monadology radically freed of categories involving number as well as of givens which affect communication by introducing an emotional element. Thoughts which would be thought as thoughts of a single mind, acts presenting themselves as acts of a single willing, causalities exercised as causalities of a single cause, and, reciprocally, thought which, without losing itself or its unity, would not cease to think in our thoughts, a willing which, without sharing itself, would pass over into our wills, a productivity which, without dispersing itself, would not cease to disturb itself, such might be an absolute unitive experience from which our unitive experiences, with their gropings, appeals, and prayers without answer and with their intermittences, are infinitely distant and of which our concrete communities are but a distant image. For us, what takes the place of this absolute unitive experience is the certitude of unity, the primary intuition which transcends our unitive experiences, which works at promoting them and introduces into their ever incomplete history something beyond history. Even in pausing, this certitude of unity arouses deeper modes of love by its exigency of unconditionality.

The advance of existence now accomplished marks a decisive transformation of the idea of person which duty supposed and reinforced. A contrast is accentuated between the person who defines himself by rational autonomy and the being who comes to himself within communication animated by unitive aspiration. The first results of this interchange of minds are beliefs and feelings which involve the innermost being. Consciousness discovers how very much autonomy, with its defensive and closed character, risked impoverishing the person. Consciousness discovers this when, opening itself to another consciousness and enriching itself with the movement of reciprocity which develops, it prepares itself not passively to resign the value of its beliefs but to agree to be confronted with different or opposed beliefs. Through this act the self reaches over toward existence. As long as the self remains alone with itself, it has no guarantee of the truth of its being. It cannot be assured that its beliefs do not reflect what within itself is most contingent or that they do not express a difference which is an obstacle to communication of minds.

The idea "rational person" issues from the desire to oppose such differences with the similarity based on common participation in the universal. But this necessary affirmation can make us think that there is no other difference than this material, empirical difference whose value reason directs us to reject. There is an ethic implied in every conception of the self. But the opposition within the self itself between reason and tendencies transfers to the person a relationship between the rational and the empirical which is familiar to theoretical thought. Then one considers as contingent with respect to reason givens which are added synthetically to it to constitute a given individuality. The difference becomes suspect in the order of value as the empirical difference with respect to the concept is lost in the irrational. The being of each person is in its participation in the universal, and the givens to which one ascribes the limits of this participation or the resistance it encounters are also those which determine and maintain the individual. Thus, the difference which enters into the structure of the self is also an element of delay which one might think is at the origin of the division of human spirits. It is incumbent, then, upon an ethic in devaluating the difference to prolong in the order of action and willing the effort of theoretical thought to create the universe of the concept and of law. If the difference is invincibly mixed in with the interchange of minds, let it be to remind them of the great value of withdrawal and neutralization of the individual and communion in the universal.

Here we recognize sufficiently the essential characteristics of an ethic whose bottom limit is a moral rationalism favorable to a juridical conception of the relations between persons and whose top limit is a mysticism of the One in which is abolished the distinction of persons which was affirmed at the level of moral action in the world only to witness to and to strengthen rational autonomy against the pretensions of individuality as such.

In opposition to this rational idea of the person, can we preserve a difference which would no longer be characterized by a negative sign and give to the person ontological quality, by which it truly becomes a spiritual subject, a metaphysical unity?

It is this path that is taken by doctrines careful to give a meta-physical status to the being of the self, whatever may afterwards be their desire to restore the ontological solidarity of persons and to found concrete communities at the specifically moral level. The seeming strength of these doctrines is made up of the impotency in which rationalism of the person finds itself when it must recognize aspirations of the self which assimilation of the person and the universal cannot satisfy. It would be useless here to undertake discussion of these doctrines. The only question for us is to know whether we can expect the communication of minds to be creative, to produce an advance of existence when one begins by giving persons a transcendent determination which does not allow their interchange to introduce into the relationship of the self with itself a difference generative of a new being.

This relationship already owes its interiority to spontaneous communication. If, afterwards, friendship, love, and confession, the absolute modes of communication, are for the self the origin of a radical progress in existence, it seems that the self, over-turning certain illusory or disappointing defenses erected for its protection, rediscovers at that moment possibilities of being born from spontaneous communication. The person does not so much have to go out of himself as to find in his own being the trace of these possibilities and the memory of the first experiences in which, as person, he was constituted as the pole of appeals and responses in which he experienced his power in affronting, af-firming, denying, and refusing. There is no one of these actions that is not inscribed in the structure of the inner being and which is not something like the cell of a possible self. The act of the person, that is, his relation to himself, envelops and concen-trates a diversity of relationships ready to be actualized in com-munication which will respond to his most secret desire and will be like a liberation for him. As the person gives up the idea of the simplicity of his being or of a subjectivity powerless to break its solitude, which he might be inclined to form of himself, he only regrasps at the depths of self the diversity of relationships which make him solidary with other minds.

However, between the moment in which subjectivity is con-stituted for itself through communication and the moment in which the self discerns that it has only to follow certain paths already traced in its being in order to restore an interchange from which it anticipates it can expect everything for its inner progress, there stands, and always will stand, the act by which, deepening the signification of solitude, the self raised itself to a certitude and an affirmation of unity from which it can no longer be distracted. When the self turns toward this certitude, when it asks from it a regeneration of its being, it dissolves all the ties which bind it to the world and to other minds. It freely annuls within the self the value it indulgently attributed to itself. A figure, instead of remaining inert, might undertake to bring itself to consciousness of self and for that reason would shed all accidental and contingent givens by which it is affected so as to grasp itself finally in its actual and permanent relationship to the law which engenders it and from which it is distinguished only as an individual expression. Likewise, the self, when it has forgone the contingent differences which in no way help it to understand itself, perceives itself as the pure figure of a pure self to which it owes its being. But the terminology of self obscures more than it illuminates the immanence in the being of the self of a generative law through which all opacity of the difference disappears.

Since there is a radical hiatus between the pure difference in the original relationship of consciousness to its source and the concrete differences which are the lot of each individual, it is necessary that these latter be given up first of all so that, redis-covered at the level of consciousness involved in the world, these differences can be freely assumed and serve real actions destined in communication to verify the primary certitude. It follows that conversion to the One must appear alternatively as the only real operation or as completely ideal and inefficacious conversion if it is not accompanied by a reciprocal promotion of existence in com-munication. Communication then appears alternatively as the only real operation or as the symbolic expression in which is manifested the impossibility of verifying in friendship and in love an intuition and a certitude which suffer no inadequation.

The being of the person is at the crossroads of this twofold relationship. It is defined by both. It is the living unity of an existence which understands itself absolutely through its source and accomplishes itself in the society of minds. If rational auton-omy is only an element of its being, even less can it be considered as an individual essence. It is always in movement, oscillating between unity, in which it understands itself absolutely, and communication of minds, in which it conquers itself as much by the acts of another as by its own acts. It was necessary to pass through duty and rational autonomy for empirical individuality no longer to be an irritant and an obstacle, for no confusion to be feared between the expansion of vitality alone and the true growth of existence. But beyond duty, and thanks to the ascesis of duty, without duty ever being forsaken, the interchange of minds conspires in the creation of the person in his twofold relationship to the certitude of unity and to individual acts by which beings make themselves as transparent as possible to one another.

The person cannot aim directly at this possession of self without its immediately escaping him. But let another consciousness, appropriating the generative intention of the movement which opens me to it, respond to my act, and it gives me infinitely more than I have been able to give it. This other consciousness places me on the path of my being. This is what was already done by spontaneous communication at the level of the first emotional exchanges. It is a different quality of being which engenders a communication purified by duty, fortified by the experience of solitude and of fault, careful not to harm the modesty of consciousness. Participation in the universal arranges possibilities of communication which are so many possibilities of existence which a rigid determination of our being would exclude. If strict moral relationships are inscribed in an ethic as a moment whose importance must not be weakened, it would sterilize them to cut them off from the source where the most affectionate exchanges are nourished. On the other hand, it would be failure to see that they are oriented toward communication which transcends the order of reason. This is why no argument is more powerfully in favor of the founding of an order based on the relationships of right and duty, in favor of the arrangement of a world corresponding to these exigencies, than that of the help which would be received by a flowering of being in an interchange of minds freed of the limitations or the servitude of desire and nevertheless free to have desire serve its highest aspiration. Nor will one doubt that, the more the specifically moral order includes communities ordered to an idea and to belief, the more favorable will it be to a communication of minds which will introduce a new depth into emotional relationships born of life itself.

Thus one can follow throughout the forms in which the relation of man with man is realized, and, under the control of reason, the passage from one moment of an ethic to another, which is nothing less than the passage from a certain idea of self to another. However, this idea includes the relation which communication institutes between minds; it cannot be disassociated from it. We take possession of our inner being only through communication or for communication and always in relationship to it. When with communication in mind we reformulate the idea of our being, the act of communication does not fail to influence this idea and transform it. Beneath the definition of man on which every ethic bases its determination of duty, without difficulty one will find the kind of communication which served as an ideal. One can be assured that the urgency of duty, no less than the neglect or the transgression of commandments in which it is expressed, contributes to retaining the definition of our being on a level which excludes both other kinds of communication and a deepening or enriching of the idea of our own being.

Confession makes all that manifest. At one time it presents itself as an act which decides for a promotion of communication and in that way for an advance of existence. At another time it regulates itself on a predetermined idea of minds which interrogate one another, and it conspires to fix and to consolidate a certain structure of our being. However, whether confession begins a progress of consciousness or delays passage to another kind of communication or, on the contrary, arranges its possibility, in no case is it indifferent to the quality of minds between which it establishes a bond. It must also reject the representation of separated minds which would be, each for itself, before confession, in possession of its inner being. Undoubtedly, this representation is favored by an imperative of veracity which allows the self no hesitation with regard to self or with regard to the quality of other minds or with regard to truth itself. However, nothing is farther from the movements and real intentions of a consciousness which prepares itself to speak the truth. It cannot disassociate the thought of its act from the thought of the consciousness which will receive the confession. The confession changes everything: the relation of the being with itself and its relationship to truth as well as its relation to other minds and to their inner being.

Certainly, in considering this form of communication in which, properly speaking, there is no longer question or answer but only transmission of truth from rational person to rational person, interchangeable one for the other, moral philosophy proceeds in conformity with a method of abstraction and generalization. It is a very precious method as long as it is important above all to oppose the interested reticence of the individual with the decisions of reason. To protect consciousness from all misunderstanding as to the quality of the motives which led it to confront the imperative of veracity and other contrary imperatives, nothing is more desirable than the fiction of a communication in which neither the quality of the being who interrogates nor the quality of the being who responds nor the idea which each has of the other modifies the nature of duty. The progress of consciousness to which this fiction corresponds marks a rupture with nature and forbids the individual to turn the game of communication to his own ends. From this point of view, it is with good reason that reason does not agree without resisting that another form of communication enter the lists, a form inspired only by respect for the universality of truth and for values of another order. In this way, the rational imperative of veracity, as does the whole order of duty, reserves possibilities of communication which might be subject to some suspicion if the intentional movements of the soul were not in this way purified.

Reason introduces itself into the interchange of minds to direct it more surely toward forms in which a meaning, which this interchange ran the risk of neutralizing, can be restored to the quality of the one who interrogates or the one who responds. Through the rational person a discernment is realized between a subjectivity whose intrusion falsifies communication and a subjectivity which is existence itself, tried and formed by communication. It is well that the self has been able to put itself in order with the exigencies of reason, for thus it feels the nostalgia for a truth of which the least one can say is that it concerns the conquest of a truth to which access can be had only through communication which no longer allows the inner being a way to hide itself or to flee. This absolute self-transparency which the self seeks and attains in its conversion to the highest certitude it must now obtain through communication having no other goal than the mutual creation of minds. These are opposed and yet complementary ways. For the more it advances in itself through communication, the more the self discovers that it is not yet equal to its being in such a way that it must rely both on the act through which it understands itself absolutely without really transforming itself and on the confession through which it really conquers itself without becoming fully transparent to itself.

On veracity almost without dialogue, and on veracity determined by concrete relations which link not only man to man but father to son, soldier to leader, friend to friend, the desire for communication is nourished which, without repudiating these relations but, on the contrary, because of their aid, allows consciousness to go beyond what is asked or expected of it. What is asked of it and what it asks, what is expected of it as well as what it expects of another consciousness, is, within the situation in which it is involved, veracity in the matter of facts or actions. What consciousness carefully watches for within this veracity is the birth of a dialogue opening up for the self a path toward itself. What it watches carefully for is the possibility of a confession which transcends initial duty, the regeneration of its inner being by a free interchange of minds. For this to happen, what is needed, besides this rational reciprocity which has it consider itself from the point of view from which it is seen by another, is that each consciousness feel itself deeply affected by the appeal which is addressed to it or by the response made to it—so deeply affected that, grasping within its own change the action of a foreign liberty which recognizes itself as incapable of realization by its forces alone, it awakens to the feeling of both its power and its dependence. The relation which it has with itself henceforth envelops a relation to another consciousness in such a way that it can no longer define its own being outside the act of this other consciousness.

The conditions of possibility of confession are fulfilled when two minds experience in solidarity that they are going, each through the other, toward the encounter of their true being, thus verifying the identity of their relationship to the highest certitude, which is certitude of unity. The consciousness which receives the confession welcomes through its act an act for which in solidarity it assumes responsibility, and it restores free disposition of its present and of its future to the self which has declared to it the truth of its past. If it does not encounter any consciousness to grasp within the expressed truth the act of an existence addressing its appeal to another existence, the self will doubt whether it can recover the integrity of its being. The authenticity of its will of regeneration is guaranteed for it only by the act of another consciousness responding to its aspiration. But how does this other consciousness respond? By the sole fact that, renouncing for self every form of superiority or of condescension, it restores the communication of minds which had been broken. What response to confession recreates is the possibility of a history, the regrasping of its history for the self which has found audience. The past act is not abolished in its materiality. But the obstacle is set aside which it had occasioned by implying in its own conditions and in its motivation the negation of the communication of minds. Nevertheless, consciousness which appropriates the generative intention of confession experiences an ennobling of its existence and a renewal of its history. It deteriorates if it remains in itself inferior to the confidence placed in it. It cannot expand its liberty in turn except by meriting and by justifying this confidence. For each consciousness its relation to another consciousness has become more interior to it than its own being.

In particular, when confession concerns a past fault, its value for the promotion of being is a function of the kind of communication to which it is bound. The self which confesses and thus assumes actual responsibility for a past responsibility aspires to free itself from itself through the act in which it declares its fault and in which it becomes, it thinks, other than the self which committed the fault. It thinks that it is freer in the act of confession than it was in the act which it confesses. But how great is its surprise when it discovers that other minds, seeing in the confession only the materiality of the fact, on the contrary identify the self which confesses with the one who was the author of the fault: the self sought communication, and the minds to which its appeal was addressed see in its act nothing but an authorization to break off all communication. Perhaps it responded to a question but receives no response from those who asked the question. Truth denounced the fault, but the act which spoke the truth was heard by no one. No consciousness gave echo to the desire for a witness, to the desire for communication. Everything changes if consciousness, which questions or listens, retaining in the confession only the appeal addressed to it and stripping away all other feeling, opens itself to communication. During this communication, by a reversal of the original situation, it will perhaps seek in the confession its own liberation in turn.

In this way we can see better why every level of communication corresponds to a determination of "Who am I, I who answer? Who am I, I who interrogate?" The meaning of lying can be understood only in relationship to these determinations. When these determinations justify a suspension of veracity, they suppress at the same time all possibility of instituting communication at a level where they could withdraw or be annulled. It is the price paid by imposed or willed transgressions of veracity required by reason: imposed when they are by the injustice of social relations, willed when they issue from an act which destroys all hope of a promotion of existence through the communication of minds. As soon as the self is no longer for itself what it wished to be for another, it can no longer think itself from the point of view from which another self thinks it with communication in view without coming upon the duality which it itself created and which deprives it of all hope of regrasping or conquering its being in unitive experiences. The interests of existence are indivisible, and truth cannot be harmed in one place without the forms of communication which touch upon deep possibilities of existence being made more difficult and more precarious. The mutual ennobling of liberties must be produced at all levels for two minds, finally attentive to each other, as though they were alone in the world, to be able to verify in their interchange the relation which each for itself has with its own source.

The promotion of minds in unitive experiences of communication thus transfers the highest certitude to the level of value. The first principle cannot be an object of knowledge. The strongest reason for refusing every assertion concerning the primary affirmation which would attempt to present itself with the authority of knowledge is that it renders useless or sterile or impossible communication whose function is on the contrary to occasion a free and progressive interpretation of a certitude of unity which is beyond all determination. If this interpretation is expressed in beliefs, it is not a similarity of beliefs one must expect from communication but the cessation of hostility between minds professing different beliefs. Unitive experiences keep the self from so confusing its being and its beliefs that it can no longer see anything but an enemy or a stranger in one who does not share them. It is not that minds uniquely curious about what they call their inner life have to avoid confronting their beliefs or their affirmations not only in matters where they cannot reject some submission to an object but in those in which interpretation is a function of strength, depth, and unitive experience. On the contrary, it seems that no communication arbitrarily deprives itself of the help of ideas or beliefs which are its matter. But the confrontation of ideas is not converted into true communication for the promotion of existences unless it succeeds in touching at some point the depths of the intimateness of being.

Therefore, there is no need to choose between communication relative to ideas detached from existence on which they feed and communication indifferent to all that does not directly cooperate in the growth of inner being. In the first case, a splitting of ideas and of the self transpires which is the greatest obstacle to growth of the inner being. In the second case, feelings seeking their substance only in themselves become anemic. Communication is decisive for the history of being only if minds in their unitive experience do not cease giving an interpretation of the highest affirmation which is more and more profound, more and more adequate for all the exigencies of the human spirit.

10 / Spiritual Forms or Virtues

AWARENESS OF OUR BEING obtained through duty, although abstract and incomplete with respect to the depths of our aspiration, still includes reflection on the relationship of our actions to our real will. Even though the self is in search of a deepening of self through unitive experiences or actions which go beyond duty, duty is a necessary test for a consciousness which questions itself about the relationship of its inner being to qualities implied in behavior ruled by the moral law. Whether the self undertakes to bend or adapt inclinations to duty, as happens in acts of virtue, or whether it seeks to be assured of the purity of its willing, it cannot avoid being in doubt. It doubts whether its act witnesses to a promotion of its being and to a true appropriation of the law or whether the law remains foreign to its being unless there is adequation between the real motivation of its act and the reason of duty. In the movement which brings the self closer and closer to itself, the moment of duty is par excellence the one in which reflection on action can instruct it concerning its true being. In this middle region of duty, a synthetic relationship is unendingly formed between desire born of natural inclination and volition controlled by law. Law either beats down or always contradicts desire sufficiently so that, by means of the distance or the *rapprochement* between its nature and its act, the self can take possession of itself in reflection.

As soon as moral intention is no longer considered in the instant in which it is efficacious, consciousness is greatly embarrassed. As soon as it is related by the subject itself to its being and it seeks in this moral intention an indication of a will whose permanent quality is found in the diversity of its expressions, consciousness is embarrassed. Consciousness cannot settle for an idea of episodic intentions, without any bond between them, nor form or accept the idea of a self endowed with qualities which would make of it a given being. There is too great a qualitative resemblance between our intentions grasped at their birth for us not to fear that they might betray our being. But just as it is easy to conceive a nature which is only nature, radically exempt from all moral qualification, so we rightly balk at characterizing the self with qualities which are copies of the value predicates by which, one by one, our actions are affected. We have no way of being sure that our correct actions add up to a reform of our being. Nevertheless, we cannot remain below our high ideal of duty without at once judging ourselves globally. It is similar to the judgment we would make of a being whose nature we would characterize while contradictorily conceiving him as having the power of free will. One would like to avoid the difficulty by taking up a position within the instantaneousness of intentions and the discontinuity of acts. In this way, we believe that both the idea of an affinity of our decisions as well as that of a growth of our value or of a progressive degeneration of our being would be excluded. But the discontinuity of our decisions is never such that it can be separated from the responsibility for self assumed by a subject which does not annihilate itself in each of them.

Faced with this question, which consciousness cannot avoid, the role of reflection is first of all to protect the self against an objective representation of its being. Consciousness loses sight of itself and separates off from itself both in constructing this representation and in giving up any concern to compare itself with itself. Undoubtedly, nothing can aid consciousness more in maintaining the purity of its intentions and in unmasking the sophisms of self-love than the fact of not only remembering the resistance which dictates that it cannot diminish its effort but also of forging the idea or the fiction of the being of a self to which it can ascribe as moral qualities, virtues or vices, the positive or negative value predicates which it ascribes to its own actions. It is not bad that we call ourselves cowardly after an act of cowardice. That way we become sensitive to and we reinstate unendingly a difference between the being which we are through our acts and the being which would have absolutely raised its desire to the level of duty and of law. But we become prisoners of a fiction, which should remain an act and a method, if we convert into permanent qualities of a self the predicates which assign value to our volitions. We naturalize consciousness without succeeding in spiritualizing nature.

Outside of *operari* we know nothing of our being except that the being which we are through our actions is not equal to the being which we aim at through them. It is the ever renewed distance between the "I am" which is at the base of our aspiration and the "I am" of our actions which results in these actions, gathered together and coordinated because of their affinity, occasioning the idea of a being of a self endowed with qualities as a cause might be endowed whose causality offered certain characteristics. Thus, the feeling of tension, between the being which we are without being able to be equal to ourselves and the being which we are because of our real actions, can be strengthened by the idea of a self which would preserve in some manner the value of our individual actions. Provided we did not objectify this self, it could usefully symbolize for us both the idea of a continuity of our being revealed as well as created by our actions and a source of permanent opposition to our highest aspiration. But the presence of the predicate should suffice to witness to the distance at which we are from the being of a self which would no longer be a being endowed with such or such quality but a pure act.

In relation and in opposition to a self which takes on substantive form, conversion to morality corresponds to a radical erasure of the predicate. However, the only guarantee we have of this conversion is our actions taken one by one. It is contradictory to seek to have these actions rely on the being of a self in which the conversion would be consolidated. We have only our intentions. The totalization of our intentions escapes us and has to escape us as long as we do not return to an *esse* more fundamental than the *operari*. It is quite true that our actions seem to us to come from an *esse*, but this is because of their opaqueness and because of their link to both docile and intransigent inclinations which resist our aspiration. A contrast, which awakens the hope of once again possessing oneself, is recreated between the promise of absolute renewal implied in a decision and the trace of our actions in memory because of the hardening which they undergo. Within this hope, or rather becoming one with it, the unconditionality of our certitude is affirmed. The *esse* which would correspond to this hope would be a completely self-transparent *operari*. It is the antithesis of the *esse* in which our past and our nature would contract and to which our qualities would cling. Between one *esse* and the other *esse*, duty is available to us. The antithesis is found there in the guise of a tension which is existence itself.

Between the person and his qualities is there not, all the same, a closer relationship, a more immediate relationship, such that operation should only be considered as the expression of the being of the self, adding nothing to it, creating nothing but revealing and witnessing only to its qualities and "virtues"? One must conclude that *operari* is subordinate to *esse* if action not only does not increase being but is worthwhile only to the extent that the person who accomplishes it is beforehand and originally worthwhile. Also, one must reach the same conclusion if the concrete being of the person manifests itself through its actions, or if, while not being substance, the person, present without losing himself in his actions, proves his identity by the qualitative direction of his intentions or if the person is originally in his nonempirical being good or bad. This position leads, however, to admitting an intuition of the power to act. It is a primary intuition like the intuition which the person has of his self and whose value, superior or equal to that of acting properly speaking, does not require real actions to be grasped by consciousness. From this point of view it is correct to call the different modes of this power virtues or qualities of the self. "The person is a continuous actuality: he has an intuition of virtue under the mode of a power of this actuality relative to what is the object of duty." [1] Thus virtues, sharing in the nonempirical character of the person, will not be confused with habits or empirically acquired dispositions. They are intuitional givens, and consciousness of this power to act is not less immediate than that of duty itself. It is an autonomous ethical category. Even more, if there is a rigorous correlation between the qualities of being of the person and the intuition he has of his moral power, of its size and its

---

1. Max Scheler, *Der Formalismus in der Ethik und die materiale Wertethik* (Bern and Munich: Francke Verlag, 1966), p. 103, note 1. [I have used the most recent edition, since the footnote in the French edition of *Eléments pour une éthique* does not list the date of publication or the publisher.—TRANSLATOR.]

limits, of what he is capable of for good or for evil, independently of all real action, and if, besides this, our judgment of other people and their qualities is based on such a judgment, then it is right to conclude, against Kant, that it is not consciousness of duty which commands consciousness of our power, that it is not the moral law immediately certain in the act in which it is posed which is the source of feeling of our power.

In order to understand the true inspiration of this doctrine, we must add that the intuition of this power is related not to the strength which we have but to the values which belong to our being and that its variations are not allied to the empirical memory of movements which accompanied our real actions. Far from becoming identified with our habits, it is the feeling of this moral power which contrives to determine them.[2] One must avoid confusing it with the possession of an aptitude; it does not pertain to an objective and explanatory psychology. One might rather say that the feeling of this power prolongs the intuition which determines differently for each person the field of values to which he has access. It does so in such a way that the primary qualities of the person, his intuition of values, and his consciousness of his moral power are only three different expressions of a single fact. Also, the feeling of our impotency relative to such an action ideally required by duty is identified with vice. This is a quality of power not subject to the initiative of consciousness.

Everything happens as if this doctrine, which so happily takes up a position against assimilation of the person with his character, would restore at another level the qualitative unity of an essence. A transcendent determinism based on the singularity of essences is substituted for, or added to, a determinism of character worked out by objective psychology. Certainly, it must be recognized that it is absurd to propose or dictate to an individual duties to which, as he sees it, no perception of values corresponds. Will one say, nevertheless, that intuition discerns in the field of values only those which are appropriate for the person? The person then knows, through this intuition, what he is, since the intuition reveals to him what he is capable of. The vocation of the person linked to the intuition of transcendent values recalls the idea of an intelligible character. Duty and the act of being are subordinated to an *esse* on which they depend for their limits.

2. *Ibid.*, pp. 129, 245.

The affirmation of such moral predestination of the person cannot be rejected unexamined by a philosophy of existence that is indifferent to every ideal which cannot stand up to the test of verification and which remains without basis in concrete reality and without some grounding in individuals. Nevertheless, what confidence can you have in an intuition of power to act which is a function before action itself of the primary qualities of the person? What means have we for reflecting on these qualities if they determine and limit the feeling of our power to such a degree that certain values, and consequently certain actions, are from the very beginning excluded from our moral horizon? What means have we for reflecting on these qualities if our vices are as fixed as our virtues by these directions of our moral intentions, if we cannot hope that action, breaking the circle in which this transcendent nature enclosed us, can restore to us the feeling of a power about which we began to doubt, and if, finally, there is constant danger of a disassociation between what we know must be done and what we know we are able to do?

Before action, how very erroneous can be the estimation we make of our power. Either we judge it to be too great or we underestimate it! How many times we accept as disaccord between our moral complexion and a given region of morality what is only the result of our cowardice! But is not this cowardice, one might say, only, in fact, experience of our impotency? Then it is this experience itself which is in question. Is it a judge of self and invariable? Not at all. Undoubtedly, one can willingly follow Scheler when he denies that this experience of unhappiness or of happiness is independent of our feelings and of our purely material pleasures; just as a feeling of buoyancy or of despair which affects the soul in its depths is not explained by conditions accessible to an objective psychology, so likewise the feeling of our moral power eludes any analysis which would make it into a resultant of elementary givens. Nothing is truer. But for that reason must one ignore the increase of moral energy, ignore the change in the feeling of our power brought about by a risk assumed by an *élan* which goes beyond what we thought possible?

The truth is that refusal to absorb the singularity of the self in the impersonal "I think" must not have, as a consequence, a determination of the moral possibilities of the person. There is no necessary tie between repugnance which the self feels toward handing itself over to reason and the intuition of a vocation expressing itself in a feeling as misleading as that of the power to act. It is not that the idea of vocation can be neglected. But it has its full meaning and is acceptable only through duty, whose universality, far from excluding vocation, protects it against the illusions of feeling either that there is in us some inclination too easily to place our virtues beyond duty or that, by a miscalculation of our power, we remove ourselves from the obligation which would free us. The opposition between duty and vocation is resolved in a fruitful tension. Whether it is found in duty or whether it promotes it, vocation can be experienced only in contact with duty, while duty, by first of all opposing vocation, purifies consciousness of rationality and deepens it. By not limiting duty with a preliminary consultation of its vocation, a consciousness has some chance of finding a duty which would be its vocation. Invention, which gives existence its depth, is already at work on the frontiers of duty.

However, after having rejected an objective representation of the self as well as a transcendent determination of his being, are episodic actions all that are left of a person? Do we love a person for his actions, or do we not rather recognize in them a quality of the self which action manifests but does not create? Do we not discern in a causality, by which a consciousness recognizes duty, a quality of this causality which is not identified with the quality of an action done in conformity with duty? Do we not see that this quality of causality spreads out, one might dare say, through all the testimony a self gives concerning itself? Are we not sometimes sure that a being is more worthwhile than its actions or, inversely, that certain isolated actions, no matter how beautiful or courageous they might be, do not prove that the self is truly at its level? Esteem and love are not based on passing acts somehow detached from the self.

What we grasp of another self is a particular rhythm of existence which is deeper than the diversity of modes in which it manifests itself. What we call nobility or purity or generosity is this rhythm or one of its forms. It is still an action but more secret than the actions which express it. We immobilize this rhythm of existence as qualities of the subject, as moral complexion. For the mobility of inner life we substitute predicates. However, the qualities in which we locate this rhythm are not aimed at by the self in which we declare them to be present. The intuition which the self has of self and the way in which it is attentive to its feelings and actions keep it from perceiving itself beneath the characteristics which we get at in it. This is because this attention is not directed to itself but to purposes and values which are intrinsically worthwhile. They are worthwhile not only in relationship to qualities which the self would like to possess. In the self we are not able to come upon the desire to acquire these qualities, which make it lovable, without immediately being put off or forbidden to ascribe them to it. We cannot think of ascribing them directly to ourselves. But the manifestation of consciousnesses in which we grasp them directs us away from certain actions and frees us from emotions and desires from which beings whom we esteem or love we see clearly are exempt. Indirectly, through the purification which it produces in us, the perception of these qualities contrives to direct our activity and to modify the rhythm of our own existence. Thus an active and loving consciousness and a consciousness sensitive to the qualities of another being are not situated at the same point of view. The first cannot adopt for itself the point of view of the second and think of the predicates by which its being is qualified without having thought which corrupts it slip into its actions. When Montaigne asks, would it not be true that in order to be entirely good we must be good "by hidden, natural and universal propriety, without law, without reason, without example," is he not trying to say, above all, that true goodness is that which, unaware of itself, shines forth in actions?

Applied to the idea of virtue, considered as a habit of morality, this interpretation of the relationship between *esse* and *operari* is faced with new difficulties. Virtue seems to involve a link with nature, and for this reason one cannot immediately see how it is possible to maintain this link without being guilty of some indulgence with respect to an objective and almost naturalistic representation of the self? One expects virtue to give a character of spontaneity to actions which nevertheless include renunciation of the interests of the sensible being. For that to happen, one supposes that morality involves itself in nature and fixes itself there as a lasting disposition. One not only asks that this disposition increase the facility of actions but that it guarantee their quality and their value. Then it is necessary for nature to be more or less consubstantial with reason and morality. This is why no moment is more favorable to the idea of virtue than that in which the role of liberty seems to be to aid in the unfolding of the powers of nature and in converting into true virtues those virtues that are latent in instinctive forces. What happens to virtue if liberty and nature are irreconcilable, if the instinctive dispositions, far from containing in embryo the moral virtues, have to serve an aspiration which goes far beyond nature? How conceive of perfect virtue when consciousness of duty introduces its impatience and its dissatisfaction into the determinations of wisdom? The relationship of duty to an affirmation of unconditionality which leaves no rest to existence causes the moderation and the rule of passions to be interiorly transfigured by consciousness of a certitude which introduces an element of infinity into the practice of morality. It is true that each virtue seeks to obtain constancy and assurance of being for the self by which it removes itself from the fluctuations and agitations of sensibility. But the call of duty endangers this delicate equilibrium in which rectitude of intention and efficacy of power seemed to be reconciled. Will not measure and harmony give way to a tension interior to each virtue as well as to the totality of the hierarchy of virtues?

The transfer to the self of a quality which is a copy of the value of its acts already denatures the relationship of consciousness to itself. How much more difficult must it not seem to give to a lasting disposition of the being, to a habit, a predicate which centers in a way the predicates of value which characterize particular actions? However, this is what we do when we set up virtues of truth, prudence, and courage, habits of the self whose causality is invested with a quality which communicates itself to operations. As soon as the self begins to view itself from outside and ascribes to its habits and its being a value which shines forth in its actions, all the more because it was not aimed at as such, it gives up self-judgment—judgment on its intentions and its operations. It speaks about itself as it would about a nature which would still merit praise or blame. It does for itself what it does not fear to do for other men when, trusting in operations which bear the mark of value, it imputes their merit more to their nature than to their liberty.

Nothing favors this view more than the idea, familiar to moral philosophy since Aristotle, of innate virtues which owe nothing to reason or to the will and which incite men to acts of courage or truth which have to be characterized as value. If these acts borrow their quality from the dispositions from which they issue, how much more do they not do so, we think, when they derive from virtues in whose formation reflected preference and choice have cooperated. It is thus that, both for the self and for other beings, consciousness ends in resting on virtue qualities affecting its operations. Afterwards it explains with this virtue both its operations and their qualities. Following this route, the self not only gives itself a false sense of security with regard to the proximate morality of its acts. It forgets that value belongs only to individual acts and to acts which were not willed with this value in mind because of self-interest. They were acts willed in view of purposes to which the self gives itself, for which it renounces itself, although by this detour its deepest aspiration is satisfied.

Undoubtedly, there is a completely formal practice of morality in which virtues seem to have their *raison d'être* in themselves, to be worthwhile in themselves independently of all concrete goals which activity might assign to itself. This formal practice of virtues is linked either to the impossibility, in which the self finds itself, of pursuing these goals or to the resistance and the obstacles which the world erects in front of a morality that is ambitious to act effectively. Virtue always seems to take first place in a world in which the ultimate duty for the self seems to be to safeguard self-esteem and to experience its own strength. But it seems that virtue, taking itself for a goal, is condemned to exhaust itself rapidly. This is all the more the case because the self, ceasing to defy the self, takes pleasure in the idea of growth of value. Detached from purposes which implement values, virtue, becoming indifferent to the matter of morality, reduces duty entirely to an intention of virtue. Quite naturally, the self, attentive to self and to its own being more than to the intrinsic signification of its acts, sees these acts gradually empty themselves of signification. At the most, the self can consider these acts as a preparation for real morality and as discipline which will aid the fulfillment of duty when the time comes. Still it must fear that a mounting and creative experience of morality might encounter afterwards in the strength of habit or nature more of an obstacle than a help. This is because it remains unintelligible that value, which must shine through in our acts, should be incorporated in our being to such a degree that we are absolved from meditating on the lack of adequation between our concrete, real act and an act in which we would be equal to the self which defines our relationship to the highest certitude. It seems indubitable that attention given to virtues alone distracts consciousness from considering the purposes whose conditions of realization they are. Such attention incites consciousness to believe that these purposes are fundamentally indifferent compared to the virtues for which they furnish only the occasion for their exercise. If virtues must be in the service of purposes, must lose themselves in a way in them and thus be dispossessed of their autonomy, it is because these purposes are the indispensable translator of value in the world. The moment at which virtues could pretend to be worthwhile in themselves would be the moment in which morality would have exhausted its task here on earth.

It is therefore necessary for virtue always to be counterbalanced by concrete action, by action in conformity with the interests of morality. When virtue is for this action and not for self, it is fully in accord with the total promotion of existence. As soon as virtue abstracts itself from intrinsically good and justified acts which it is called to serve, it permits what is pharisaical and hollow to show in its own idea. As soon as it makes itself solidary with its acts, it truthfully constitutes itself in this relationship and through this relationship. What the acting subject demands of itself, in fact, is to be, in view of these acts and for these acts, what, in view of these same acts, a pure spiritual subject would be who was at the same time endowed with strength and who would find in his motives and in his strength an intention and a power exactly appropriate for the quality and the nature of the acts required by duty. The idea of virtue is defined by the possibility of equating these intentions and this strength with the value of acts and with their intrinsic finality. The idea of virtue and the inquietude of virtue disappear when the act of virtue is at its highest, that is, at the moment when the intentions and the strength of the self are in accord with the actions which concrete duty expects of it. By means of intentions no less than by means of strength, the idea of virtue sends us back to a relationship of the real subject to a spiritual subject and to the desire of an adequation to be obtained between the real intentions of the acting being and its strength, on the one hand, and, on the other hand, actions destined to promote the morality of existence.

What the objective representation of a moral nature hides is the thought of a suppressed difference between the pure subject and the concrete being. As long as the distinction between liberty and nature is not made, as long as moral liberty could be considered as a kind of superior nature, virtue had in fact to pass for the highest moment of morality. It establishes or re-establishes an order contradicted or troubled by a sensibility which is not fundamentally irrational. It institutes a true nature which one can expect to inspire and command acts in conformity with those which express the rational necessity of the universe. By informing nature, reason and virtue enter in a way into possession of their rights. Just as, finally, nature and reason coincide, so virtue and duty tend to become one and to join together in being.

The problem is quite different if, for the subject, morality is tied to the renewed initiative of a liberty which finds in nature only a precarious foundation and would renounce itself by seeking to involve itself in nature in which it would lose itself. It is virtue which restrains itself so that it may remain in a living relationship with liberty and recreate a difference between a morality which seems constituted in the being of the self and a morality called to regenerate itself unceasingly while regenerating the self. Here we rediscover the metaphysical locus of all relationships between the acting being and value. It is not permissible to proceed from a predicate of liberty applied to this or that individual action to the affirmation of free causality, substantially so and such in its own being. Likewise, it is not legitimate to see in the predicate of this or that virtuous action the indication of the causality of an acting being to whom this predicate might belong as a permanent quality.

A free action as well as a courageous action or a truthful word is an action on which we confer a predicate which adds, to what this action is in its materiality, a quality attesting that we establish a positive relationship between this action and a value. But what is beneath this value if not the idea and the position of an absolute act which each concrete decision must symbolize without pretending to be adequate to it? Therefore, I am free and can declare myself free in the same way that I am virtuous and can declare myself virtuous. The two predicates express two relationships of my real being to two values, one of which always founds me as a spiritual subject while the other assigns a particular direction to morality. The relativity of the relationship of my real decision to the value which founds its predicate keeps me, not only from confusing the liberty and generosity of which I am capable with the pure intellectual or moral action whose expression they are, but from making of them qualities of the acting being or of its causality. The being of the self is in the relationship which it institutes between its real actions and values. Its virtue is this relationship.

From this point of view, when the relationship of action to value is characterized by a negative sign, logic would have it that, beginning with a predicate attesting that a virtue had been badly known or betrayed, one should not go further in the evaluation of the causality of the acting being than one thinks one is authorized to go for a predicate characterized by a positive sign. Logic would also have it that one limit oneself then to thinking that the subject deserted value by a decision without deep roots in the causality or in the *habitus* of the acting being. But the same law which had us give a kind of moral substantiality to the self incites us in the opposite sense to realize in the subject the antithesis of value and to transfer to the being of the self a negative predicate, thus misunderstanding, to the great detriment of consciousness, the relationship which constitutes it. No more than virtues can vices be separated from the moving relationship of our decisions to value. Liberty in evil is no longer so mysterious if one gives up confusing liberty and slavery, which the positive or negative predicates of our actions translate, with the judgment without predicate on which value and our hope of liberation are based.

Indeed, the idea of virtue corresponds to a hope for liberation. Each virtue specifies this hope in its relationship to temporal multiplicity, to the discontinuity of acts as well as to desires which arise from the inclinations of nature. The relationship of *esse* to *operari* here presents itself in the idea of continuity. The assimilation of virtue to a habit considered as a bond between the plurality of separated actions tends to make of continuity the character of a lasting disposition of the individual who preserves and consolidates morality in intervals when it is not in action. Progress in morality becomes allied to force of habit instead of being sought in the increased demand for purity in intention and motivation. One thinks that, the more habit draws away from the initiatives which gave birth to it and tends toward lack of self-attention in a noncreative duration, the more it assures moral action of efficacy. But Aristotle himself, even though he made habit the preliminary condition of virtue ruled by wisdom, did not believe that one could separate habit from choice or from the intellect. Nevertheless, by bringing virtue closer to the intelligible, he fixed it in a finite perfection excluding the mobility of becoming, failures, and new attempts. In the twofold way in which virtue participated in habit and in the intelligible, it tended to procure stability and fulfillment of its powers for being.

The kind of disfavor which colors the idea of virtue in philosophical literature is due undoubtedly to this certitude that, if it is permissible to conceive of a progress of consciousness, it can no longer be against time but with the help of time no less than with its resistance. In what way can virtue capture time while continuing to be ascending and creative morality? The reading of our moral experience is linked to temporal structures, and virtue corresponds to one of these structures. Even more, virtue institutes one of these structures. There time directs itself to a form which makes lovable, and polarizes, our thoughts, feelings, and actions. No matter how disparate their content, time introduces into their successive diversity a qualitative unity, a single inspiration. It is not a continuity of unforeseeable growth in duration nor a continuity of consolidation in habit but a continuity founded on the internal resemblance of acts which express one design, one will to existence, one fidelity. Liberty, of which we are capable, can be considered as a form enveloping the multiplicity of our decisions, but as itself ordained to the pure action of the spiritual subject. Likewise, virtue, as dynamic and active form, is relative to the temporal multiplicity which it tries to master. On the other hand, virtue expresses the action of the spiritual subject interior to the pure idea of veracity, of courage, or of friendship. This is why some tension, revelatory of resistance, delays, and impatience, is never excluded from the temporal continuity born of this form.

This resistance is determined for each virtue by the psychological modes of desire, emotion, and fear. A single active relationship must master these modes for itself and make them serve the self and its design. It does so more, perhaps, by annexing the energy of an inclination than by constraining or repressing it. A virtue is a spiritual form sufficiently efficacious to regulate interiorly an inclination in such a way that, instead of being an obstacle to, or getting in the way of, our aspiration to be, this inclination becomes its strongest help. The two characteristics which are found in each virtue, to give it its militant stride and its caution, relate as well to the inclination which is both utilized and contained. Virtues cooperate in the promotion of existence by working to produce in desire, emotion, love, and in pleasure itself a transmutation of meaning. If the emotions of depression and withdrawal are mastered, all that is expansive in the others rallies to the form of a willing, of a feeling interiorly in agreement with the exigencies of value. But it is at different levels that the active being experiences this spiritual form which, like a category, envelops a moving diversity of feelings and decisions. Just as the temporal continuity is not exempt from intermittences and crises, so the unity of being which virtue seeks to institute is never so sure of itself that it does not have to deal with the rebel movements of sensibility. What is not at all in doubt is that, at the height of this experience, the docility of desire to the form is such that the self, moving without effort from consideration of itself, from the idea of qualities belonging to a subject, senses itself to be fully in the actuality of feelings and of decisions which devotion to moral purposes evokes.

The rivalry or the opposition between diverse conceptions of ethics comes down undoubtedly to the rivalry of spiritual forms. None of them tolerates that virtues should be in some way autonomous and indifferent to the unity of affirmation which gathers them together, organizes them, and institutes between them relationships of dependence and, above all, has them communicate through similarity of inspiration. The problem of the unity of virtue must be resolved in this perspective. It is quite true that virtues imply one another, not in the sense that they allow themselves to become this or that fundamental virtue, but because in a single consciousness all virtues order themselves with respect to a spiritual form which is their generating schema. Each virtue locates itself with respect to this schema. Each virtue is evoked by it and endowed henceforth with a justification which allows us to integrate it into a total idea of action.

When we meditate on Socrates, Jesus, or Spinoza, it is a spiritual form which we sense and which we seek to attain. It is not without reason that the affinity or the solidarity of this form and of affirmations of the theoretical order incites us to discover a more hidden unity or center which expresses itself both in religious intuition and in a system of virtues. It follows from this that neither the virtues taken together, nor each virtue taken in isolated fashion, have their full meaning either in a doctrine or in a man aside from a spiritual form which in turn is inspired by an idea or by a certitude commanding the whole of an ethic. Only on this condition is there a morality. There is a morality only because of the difficulties and conflicts unavoidably aroused by this idea and this form when they encounter either particular dispositions of the acting being or life or society which reject or contradict them.

It is a vain enterprise to transmit morality by breaking it up, by dividing it, by dispersing it into a multiplicity of duties or virtues which are not suffused, which are not worked through, by a single aspiration. For consciousness to be is to verify that its highest certitude influences the humblest virtues and duties and does its work incognito. These virtues and these duties supplement the act in which the highest certitude should find its authentic expression. Truthfully, it is the idea of this act which gives duties and virtues their value and makes their continuity and their imperative character the symbol and expression of an affirmation which goes beyond them. The spiritual form commanding the virtues mediates this affirmation in its relationship with the time of consciousness and the multiplicity of efforts whose rhythm it regulates from within. But these efforts are themselves linked to purposes allied to society and the world in which these values are integrated. They are linked in such a manner that the coordination of virtues and duties rests finally on their common subordination to the primary affirmation.

To this we must add that, if we cannot, all the same, slight duties which accompany militant virtue, consciousness in that way nevertheless opens up a route for itself toward a region where, becoming less and less dependent on the world, it has the experience of an existence whose burden of desire is lightened. Such an action does not suppose an evasion outside the circle constituted by the relationship of the primary affirmation to the world. For the acting being who has arrived at the limits of what is possible, this action is the experience of a recurrence of the highest certitude, in which neither desire nor fear nor regret, nor the obligation of using the detour of purposes and of duties, nor transactions with the world, nor successes nor failures succeed in altering the perception of its accord with its being. If the self can never give up the effort to appropriate the certitude which is at the origin of all value by incorporating it in its tasks and in its actions, at least it now becomes attentive to a purer light, in which its feelings and all things belonging to the world bathe. The tendencies of the acting being are not wiped out. But the edge of desire is blunted in such a way that each tendency, perfectly docile to the aspiration it should serve, becomes self-transparent, as if our experience consisted henceforth in a simple exchange of the tendency with itself. As much as it is possible to affirm it, consciousness is now beyond pleasure and suffering. Its experience regenerates itself without being exposed to the vicissitudes which touch the activity of the subject in the world. While the militant virtues cannot be disassociated from the value of the purpose which they serve so importantly that this value cannot diminish without the signification of the effort being interiorly menaced, the spiritual form of the experience, on the contrary, envelops a quality of feelings which no longer varies as the level assigned to activity varies. If one wants to see virtue only where there is some tension or some effort of consciousness to have the value of the finality which is the matter of duty and the self-mastery required of the subject correspond, one can say that virtue dies the moment the level of purposes is transcended to give way to a certitude of being which without effort actualizes the relationship of consciousness to its source and its law.

Nevertheless, in another sense, this moment is also that in which virtues unfold which, although less strictly allied to purposes and duty, only reveal all the more the relationship of *esse* to *operari*. They are ordered to a fundamental virtue which is openness of heart, a disposition to recognize values different from those for which we ourselves battle, an aptitude for perceiving the complexity of moral situations in which the fortune of people is decided. The promotion of values is real only if it is accompanied by the correlative creation of spiritual forms which become for consciousness the norm of its judgments and its affirmations. In this way the idea which is at the center of all these analyses is verified. It is indeed on a single and identical act that depend, correlatively, the value inscribed in individual actions and the virtue which appropriates them. However, this act, which is source and common origin, cannot get hold of itself directly. It must divide and consent to a kind of inner breakup. On the one hand, this act incarnates itself as value in actions whose materiality allows an inspiration of another order to shine brightly within them. On the other hand, this act orients and guides consciousness, which is in quest of values. This act judges these values and thus acquires for itself a virtue, not by aiming at itself, but by aiming at actions and feelings in which these values shine forth. Therefore, it is not surprising that the highest virtues exclude any question which the self might want to pose concerning its being or the qualities it has. It is contradictory for a spiritual intention, turned toward acts and feelings, inspired by nobility and generosity, to turn back to itself to see these values issuing from its own act. This spiritual intention feels it is nothing in the promotion of value, which it grasps as a quality of actions or of persons to which it is attentive. It is unaware that it is itself the fire from which the light that suffuses things emanates. When this spiritual intention reflects on things, it is not to find some merit for itself but to relate everything to the act and the source from which derive both the quality of its power or its virtue and the quality of the actions and efforts or their value.

Thus, it is in a twofold sense that the limits of the appropriation of values are drawn. On the one hand, the actions which support values are not those we would dream of doing if it were permitted to aim directly at their realization. On the other hand, if it is certain that these actions react on the being who accomplishes them, the correlation between their value and the quality of the acting subject is not such that this quality can be willed as such. The growth or the diminution of being which the self experiences in its relationship to the values of action proves sufficiently that the way in which values react on the agent, or, if you will, the way the agent appropriates these values, does not consist in the obtaining of a quality for which its being would become the support.

Undoubtedly, the values of action affect otherwise than do other values the idea which the subject has of itself, for example, the values of beauty linked to the production of works of art. The command with which these values are solidary is such that the refusal or the adherence of consciousness implies a more direct relationship than anywhere else between the quality of action or its value and the quality of the consciousness which pronounces itself on this value. One has some difficulty in disassociating the quality of the action, effectively accomplished, and the quality which, through this action, belongs to the interior being or which this action presupposes in it. Nevertheless, consciousness spontaneously performs this disassociation. What consciousness becomes for itself through the accomplishment or nonaccomplishment of an action endowed with value or required by duty has nothing in common with the acquisition or the loss of a quality for which the self would be a support, in the way that actions are the support of values. The experience which consciousness has of the privation or the increase of being is nothing less than the experience of the moving relationship which it sustains, by the detour and the necessary mediation of its actions, with the pure self which is at the foundation of its fundamental certitude.

This relationship includes a certain choice and a secret law of preference in the appropriation of values. Only gradually does consciousness decipher their signification. The first steps of moral experience must raise us first of all to the level of universal morality. It is necessary for duty to injure, to a certain extent, our empirical being for us to be assured afterwards that our preferences are not to be confused at all with the reactions of a given nature. On the condition that we apply ourselves unendingly to disassociating empirical individuality from the self which tends toward morality, there is no incompatibility between universal values and the intimateness of a choice which finds its place among others. A form of individual existence which aspires to form our whole empirical being designs itself in our admiration and in our repugnance. Then can be born and strengthened the feeling of inadequation, even of disaccord, between the being which would correspond fully to this form of existence and the being which our actions verify. But we must guard ourselves against a feeling in which we risk lying to ourselves. If its true will is worth more than its history, no consciousness can affirm this true will for itself unless another consciousness first of all in its love in some way authorizes it to do so. The clairvoyance of love alone is permitted to discern the possibilities of existence which circumstances did not permit consciousness to actualize, the possibilities that situations and resistance interior to the being itself kept it from translating into deeds. There is nothing more hollow and more illusory than to judge oneself superior to one's actions and their mark on the world. The sketch of the inner being which we constitute distracts us from action which would give us a surer way to judge ourselves.

However, not everything is false in the feeling of an inequality of our being with itself. It has its source in the relationship of subjectivity to the source of all value. Thus, no one can entirely avoid the experience of this inadequation. It is not wrong that we allow ourselves to be guided by it in the choice of values and of goals. Although action both hides from us and reveals to us our true being, there is no other remedy for the restlessness which the feeling of this inadequation may arouse. Nothing is more disappointing than heroism which is exalted in a vacuum, in the profession of a spirituality which does not go outside the limits of language, which is exalted in the kind of inner lie which is insensibly entertained by thought nourished on the highest models of culture and history but which does not go beyond pure enjoyment of them. When thought awakens from this dream in which all value was only borrowed, it is troubled. Thought searches for itself, as does humanity in general when trial finds it weak or cowardly, a humanity which esteemed itself so highly because it saw itself through the prism of the works of the human spirit. When this happens, it begins to doubt whether these works have really cooperated to increase its value or if they have not rather hung a kind of curtain between the being whose idea it forged and its real being.

11 / Sources of Veneration

IF THE REALIZATION of liberty in the advance of existence and the movement of aspiration could satisfy the demands
of the unconditional affirmation and exhaust the relationship
which constitutes us, this exact correspondence between action
and its idea would signify that real consciousness, through its
operations in the world, had reached the same point of disposses-
sion and renunciation of self which reflective consciousness attained in its regressive movement toward its source. Through
this progress of being, liberty would no longer be only the witness to the pure subject in the history of consciousness. It would
abolish the difference between this consciousness and its source.
However, no individual consciousness can pretend to this adequation for itself. The refusal for itself of a predicate of value is
the refusal by the self for the self of a quality which would make
one suppose that the self had become equal to itself or to its
being. Through this refusal, the self reaffirms as much as it
verifies its relationship to pure consciousness of self. It protects
itself against the temptation and illusion of thinking that
through its actions it has become the subject of a real morality.
Faced with itself, a stranger both to discouragement and pride,
consciousness summons up as much of its courage as it can. It
becomes particularly attentive not to confuse discourse on action
with action itself. It defies both an ethic which recommends that
it consent to the predicate and an ethic which suggests that it
not consent to it. It still fears in this latter an excessive preoccupation with the opinion which the self could form of itself.

While refusing to accept that it is the being of the qualities

[179]

one might be tempted to attribute to it or which it might be inclined to attribute to itself, the self brings its attention back to this idea that these qualities are only the trace or the fixed image of an act which calls for and constantly awaits its renewal. The certitude which sustains this act and the refusal for self of the predicate of value illuminate and confirm each other. The judgment without predicate, which is at the source of all value predicates in individual actions, must change over for the self into an interdiction which forbids it to think that it has truly become the subject or the possessor of this or that quality. By guarding itself against all self-approbation, consciousness also maintains its relationship to the original affirmation. It guards itself against the contradiction into which it would fall if it considered itself as a being to which this or that predicate belonged. On the contrary, each of these predicates only refracts for an instant, for a liberty involved in the world, its fidelity to the pure subject.

Sometimes one sees thought incline toward the idea of the radical impotency of morality in the world. It is not uncommon for a spiritual interpretation to veil the work of real forces and for there to be more sincerity among the realists of action, attentive to the correct calculation of resistance to be overcome, than there is among moralists who aim at a kind of triumph of morality in the world where morality cannot pretend to show itself without at once betraying itself and its source. The error is equal on both sides, and it would be no less wrong to think that the success of morality can only be relative. Both opinions forget that there is no progress in the sense of growing adequation, as if the distance could be diminished between the reality which we construct with our actions, or rather between our actions themselves, and the principle which inspires them. It is a principle which always requires new actions in which we can verify that this principle is not something like a force manifesting its effects. We hold the light which illuminates our actions, but not the force.

Pure consciousness of self commands all and is capable of nothing. Therefore it is absurd to think that it is impossible for the principle of morality to succumb under the pressure of the world which denies it. There is neither failure nor success for that which carries its highest guarantee within itself and in its act. But that the ideas into which this fundamental certitude

passes and where it circulates and which are already its organism should be involved in experience and its resistance is what
makes metaphysical indifference to success solidary with com-
mitment and the will to obtain it. The refusal of the predicate is,
therefore, through the act of attention which must not be lacking, the warning which the self gives itself not to take seriously
the idea that it has effectively incorporated into its being the
unconditional affirmation which is at the source of its effort.

But will not this refusal bring with it a too facile self-pardon? If it is refusal of positive qualities by the self and for the
self, will it not equally be refusal of negative qualities? It would
seem that if the approbation interior to the decision must not
last beyond the act and become fixed as a state of consciousness,
condemnation of self within the act should not last beyond the
act. Thus, refusal of the predicate would even more easily be a
lessening of the fault than a protection against self-satisfaction.
The bitterness of memory would be spared us in exchange for
renunciation of all self-complacency. In reacting against the
empirical memory of what we have done and which condemns
us, does not the refusal of the predicate invite us to wipe out this
memory and refuse all identification of our being with the quality of its action?

However, fidelity of consciousness to its source acts here in
the same way, even though in a different direction. When this
fidelity translates itself by refusal of a predicate which would
make of the self the subject of a quality, consciousness realizes
that the act of its liberty must not be considered as susceptible of
consolidating itself in a nature. However, when this fidelity
obliges the self not to succumb to the weight of empirical memories, consciousness says that it must behave with relationship to
what, in it, is nature, as if this nature could be taken up by
liberty, not effaced, but on the contrary maintained to nourish
the flame which gradually consumes the being. If this nature
were not maintained, consciousness could not be assured that it
is not the being it was. It is through this resistance, conserved
and saved, that consciousness protects itself against the predicate which would see it condemned and no longer master of
itself and of its judgment. Thus the moving equilibrium in which
consciousness holds itself, keeping itself from self-denigration
and from pride, makes it renew its pledge while verifying that its
effort cannot carry it to the level of the primary certitude. How-

ever, as the whole of the experience of consciousness concentrates itself in each of its decisions, its serenity passes over into its effort, and its effort generates serenity. If, finally, serenity wins out decidedly over effort and invades consciousness, it is that about which the latter cannot decide but about which sometimes it has a kind of presentiment.

The very fact of being, related by consciousness to the primary affirmation, is sufficient to arouse in the self the feeling of an inequality with itself. Because of this, the act by which consciousness reconstitutes its empirical memories and the orientation it gives to this reconstitution are for it the means not only of again having the experience of this inequality but also of becoming reconciled with it, of reconstituting the integrity of its inner being, of summoning up its hope. The self makes the act by which it appropriates the memories in this manner into the support for intensifying the certitude of a single origin for all decisions in which it has understood the constitutive law of its being. When, finally, the self is no longer permitted any real action, and when it must resign itself to making its new hold on its empirical memories the instrument of self-possession through entirely internal acts, the interchange in which the self engages with itself allows it to form and encourage hope, a hope fused with the assurance of a growing victory obtained over the initial opacity of its empirical being.

The attention of consciousness to its past becomes the act by which it regrasps at a new level the certitude which directed all its effort. Dispensed from spreading its action in the world, freed through it from all that is invincibly troubling in action itself, consciousness can bring to its memories the self-attention their realization requires. These memories lie before consciousness like a text to which one must find the key and the interpretation if consciousness wants to obtain the degree of serenity which can be attained by a being which has not been able to attain full realization but which can subsequently retrace the route which this realization has taken. It can discern the necessities mixed in with the purest resolutions and have this free appropriation of the past become, to a greater degree than was possible before, the instrument of the primary affirmation. While thus interrogating its past, consciousness not only stands in opposition to that movement and that natural bent of thought which catalogues all that is accomplished as determinism. On the contrary, consciousness also assumes responsibility for self, so that the actions by which it has truly added something to the primitive nucleus of its nature, and this nature itself, become quasi-indiscernible to an attentive pure consciousness of self. As far back as the self goes in the perspective opened on its past, it sees itself incapable of sorting out clearly in its actions what expresses the unconditional demand by which it is inspired and what translates the very foundation of the being which it did not create. However, in its refusal to separate, in its becoming, what belongs to nature and what belongs to its liberty, the self verifies once again its desire to be worthwhile. The self employs its empirical memories to grasp in them, through reflection, an affirmation which transcends all of them.

Nevertheless, no consciousness can avoid asking itself whether destiny has not spared it the experience of finding itself in situations where it would have had to face conflicts which would have crushed it or torn it up. Also, consciousness must ask itself whether it has not fled situations which would have required it to really witness to its belief. Consciousness can and must have recourse to historical examples of moral sublimity which contrast the experience of nonfulfillment of its ambition with an irrefutable proof of what is at the origin of its effort. Consciousness must do this so as not to weaken beneath the weight of memory to the point of giving up subsequently all growth of value. It must also do this in order to compensate for and to maintain that diffuse feeling of fault which is born from the very fact of still being alive. Consciousness does this after having heard within its depths so many appeals which invited it to accept its ruin. But it did not listen to them. The attempts the self has made to reduce the ever renewed distance between word or writing and authentic action justify as much as they increase the feeling that examples of moral sublimity inspire. History presents these examples to the self more or less deformed by the staleness of a spirituality which weakens their witness or by the misunderstanding of a history which would believe it betrayed its realism by avowing what transcends it. By restoring the correct signification of these examples, and even in freely choosing one of them and concentrating on that all its power of adherence, consciousness, not forgetting to be moved by the generative principle of value, recreates the idea of an infinite difference between its own advancement and the consciousness in which moral sublimity breaks forth through an adequation obtained between the law of their being and their concrete action. What consciousness knows it has not attained, what it refuses to think it can obtain, it declares other minds have attained. It affirms that these minds have absolutely verified the fundamental certitude through the life they have renounced. These minds have manifested in the world and through the world an adequate image of the supreme law. The obfuscation of the generative principle of value increases the signification of these moments of the history of the world in which a being, consuming itself radically in the service of the law, converts resistance to the law into an exact symbol of the law.

Does consciousness have a sufficient guarantee of its affirmation? Is there not in this affirmation the expression of a belief and a faith which goes beyond what the givens and the facts authorize? Why, in the presence of these actions, does consciousness abandon, not only the exigencies of the explanation which allowed it to have these actions come under the common laws of nature, but even the rules of understanding which would roll back indefinitely the boundaries of understanding through motives, without placing us finally in the presence of what is ineffable in these particular actions? While remaining itself infinitely below beings which inspire it with the feeling of sublimity, why does consciousness affirm that in these beings an absolute verification of the generative principle of value is effected? Is there not a contradiction between the idea of a pure subject and the possibility that there are either actions which faithfully symbolize it or concrete minds who abolish within themselves the real difference which separates them from their source?

It is precisely the identity of our inner being and the supreme principle which lifts the contradiction by authorizing us to affirm —even more, by requiring us to affirm—the actuality of what can be for us only a hope. This identity is that at which a consciousness arrives which freely abstracts, in reflection, from what is added to pure difference to constitute the concrete being that is solidary with nature. The desire which arouses the real unfolding of existence is the desire to reabsorb through action itself what is the very condition of action and without which action would have no meaning. Therefore, nothing authorizes us to conclude, from our powerlessness, the impossibility of this victory, which is for us only an idea, that is, an infinite exigency. What meaning would the confession of our weakness have if we could not measure it with particular actions in which moral sublimity breaks forth in history, if we did not have in veneration the means of always restoring the feeling of our inequality with ourselves? It is not an assurance which can claim some objective verification; it is not a faith or a belief which can be weakened or denied by experience. The affirmation of absolute actions is at the level of history the copy of the unconditional affirmation which is at its source. We become the witnesses— even more, the guarantors—of moral sublimity.

We do not think that these absolute actions are freed of all relationship to nature and the world. Quite to the contrary, for us they are the living image of a link of consciousness with the world in which nature and life, far from causing the failure of an adequation of action and its source, are its instruments. Through these actions a twofold accord of liberty is effected, with the principle which inspires it, and with nature, on which it draws for its power to act. From this twofold point of view the antinomy of liberty and its inner principle, no less than the antinomy of liberty and natural necessity, appear subsequently relative to the modalities of effort which characterize the appropriation of values at different levels to which existence raises itself. At no moment is this appropriation so complete, so easy, or so direct that it does not include some tension, either between the act of choice and the value which must be its content or between this same act and the solicitation of nature. It is this double tension which is the very heart of the movement of liberty in the accomplishment of the possibilities of existence. It can realize itself only by renouncing itself in favor of the value which gives it content. However, this renunciation itself still envelops an initiative in which some resistance, coming from inclinations or from emotion, erupts. As tendencies come to agree with the appropriation of values and become more docile, the initiative of consciousness no longer knows itself in the emotion which it must overcome but in the emotion born of its encounter or its harmony with the primary certitude. The idea of a consciousness capable of absolute actions is at the end of this movement, and our feeling of sublimity is its expression.

It seems to us that such a consciousness does not so much choose the highest value or the most complete sacrifice as it experiences its attraction. As far as nature is concerned, consciousness does not so much have to conquer it as welcome its help and support. Consciousness forgoes the power of an always possible rebellion against the law, with which it would reserve for itself some independence with respect to the highest principle of value. Far from fearing the resistance of emotion, in which it did not cease to experience its dependence with respect to inclination, consciousness finds in it a docile auxiliary. This effacement of the twofold function which liberty exercises in each of us coincides with an exaltation of the power of liberty. By renunciation, liberty realizes itself; by aiding nature, it helps it participate in a new reign. In this combined effort of liberty and nature nothing takes place which could make one think of a victory won with difficulty by the first over the second.

In contrast, we never cease experiencing in our depths the power of an unvanquished nature and the torrent of emotions which our individual attachment to life arouses. The feeling of sublimity is born of this opposition felt in the depths of our soul in the presence of certain beings and certain actions. If these actions increase the experience of our weakness, they also contribute, more than we could have with our own resources, to regenerating in ourselves the feeling of moral sublimity. It is therefore in ourselves that the sources of the feeling of sublimity are found. We remain insensitive to the grandeur which shines forth around us if we do not participate in the source of this grandeur, if, finally, there is no identity between what we are and this source. However, since this identity in us converts into a desire to reduce through action the difference between our given being and our absolute being, we might, because of our weaknesses, come to doubt our innermost truth if we were not reminded by the absolute actions which rise up in history and offer us the pure image of what we are. In these actions the obfuscation of the generative principle of value finds an ultimate verification, for resistance to desire is there raised to the level of an instrument of expression entirely docile to consciousness. Certain beings reveal themselves as the organs of the highest principle through the sublimity of their actions. The exaltation of consciousness which they manifest to us does not contradict, but rather fulfills, the law which brings into solidarity at all levels the world and the desire to be.

There is no reason to think, however, that without these

absolute witnesses we would be absolved from duty or that it would have been permissible for us to appreciate the advance of our effort with greater indulgence or that the revelation it presents to us is the indispensable mediator between our consciousness and the primary affirmation. There is no reason to consider these witnesses as adapted to minds more sensitive to examples and to images than to a purely rational certitude. This is not the true function of moral sublimity. No more than moral sublimity conditions consciousness of the first principle, as though one could not reach the latter except through the former, is it a secondary or subordinate form or equivalent of the highest certitude. Moral sublimity is in itself fully accessible in its true import only to minds which have already experienced in effort the different moments of the realization of the desire to be. It is this experience alone which prepares consciousness for the intuition of moral sublimity. The surplus of confidence it experiences does not bear so much on the primary affirmation as on its relationship to the world and to value. The feeling which it acquires and which influences all its earlier experience and penetrates its new experiences mixes a kind of repose or security with its hope.

What is the relationship between these absolute actions and the generally accepted forms of human grandeur? These forms are the categories of moral sublimity. They do not so much seem to separate off from history as to dominate and regulate it. It is as though these forms were the inner laws of acting consciousness, regulative of its feelings and its thoughts, such that the historical figures in which we grasp them only illustrate them rather than contrive to create them. Each of these figures would be an example, a variation on a fundamental theme with respect to these categories of the sublime. The example should aid us to take possession of the idea of the type. Afterwards, we might compare the example to this idea; with it we might measure its value. In this sense there would be *a priori* forms of human grandeur, limiting and determining the modes of its production. Strictly speaking, no example could be equal to them.

If, speaking in this manner, one wants to say that there is no consciousness which can pretend for itself to have responded to the exigencies of one or the other of these forms and to the idea which it has of them which can inspire its behavior, nothing is surer, nothing more evident. But nothing is more incompatible with intuition of the sublime than this comparison which we are asked to make between the idea and the fact. It is much more correct to think that these categories of the sublime have been set down in the course of history by creative action, whose wake they are. There are as many matrices of grandeur as one can count historical moments in which the sublime broke forth in this or that individual action, in this or that life. These forms which gradually take on a transhistorical or suprahistorical character have an available origin in existences in which one cannot disassociate, other than by abstraction, actions and the doctrine whose expression they are. It is precisely the reciprocal envelopment of doctrine and actions which arouses in us the feeling of the sublime through the impossibility in which we find ourselves of disassociating word and act. The foundation of grandeur in every order is this unity of doctrine and life borne to a point where one no longer knows which of the two engenders the other.

Consequently, one should not be surprised by the affinity discovered between witnesses to the same force of grandeur or by doctrinal affinities which bring them close to one another. Relations and affinities reveal their common relationship to an identical origin. Even though the doctrine deepens and is renewed, even though individuals in different historical circumstances witness differently to their fidelity, one can recognize sufficiently a single inspiration. But nothing more is needed for thought immediately to conceive of a type or a structure from which individual minds do not stray. Then one is on the way to the ideal which admits all weaknesses because it has been separated from the origin in which doctrine and action were fused. One is inclined to attribute to the operation generative of the form which it leaves behind only the signification of an example with respect to this form. One forgets that there would be neither form nor example if in these individual moments of history there had not been creation of form and action at the same time.

But, could one not ask, can one not see that each form of grandeur unites and coordinates values, feelings, and dispositions of the soul in which a single inspiration moves in such a way that creative action at the level of history seems to have it as a mission to verify this inspiration, to find its eternal signification, to give it new luster? Is it not apparent that each form of grandeur orders to itself all the inner movements of consciousness? Of what is our idea of holiness, of heroism, or of wisdom made if the varieties which each can present of these forms are so numerous? Do we not recognize in each the predominance of a central value or the attraction which it wields over the feelings and inclinations of the soul? As different as forms of wisdom can be, do we not find ourselves in the company of a will to harmony, a taste for lucidity, for clairvoyance, for self-mastery even in consent to palpable joys and to nature? As different as the forms of heroism can be in the service of various goals, do they not manifest the same generosity, the same attraction of sacrifice? It is even much easier to recognize in the forms of holiness, despite all that differentiates them, the predominance of renunciation, purity, humility, and fidelity to a divine model. Therefore, there would be, anterior to it, intrinsic affinities between qualities of the soul, or virtues, and groups of values which one might consider in themselves, apart from historical examples which illustrated them.

We would not want to deny that there are spontaneous feelings of the human soul enjoying harmony. But there is a great distance between the natural alliances enjoined between dispositions of the soul and the wisdom we know to be that of Socrates or Goethe, the holiness we know to be that of St. Francis of Assisi or of Jacqueline Pascal. What is fascinating in each of these people is the unity of doctrine and act. It is a singular combination of values, none of which remains isolated from the others which sustain it or from the real operations of consciousness which verify it or from the thought which guarantees and prolongs its signification. We do not hesitate to say that it is these minds which, by their own act, have occasioned this solidarity of virtues and doctrine which afterwards remains for us an ideal form half-detached from history and transcendent to it. In vain would one want to separate these forms of grandeur from the historical moment of their appearance. In vain would one want to be unacquainted with the doctrine which they envelop. It is the unfolding of the inner idea of the acts which witness to it.

Rationalist wisdom, with the order of values and virtues which give it its own character, also has an ethicohistorical character when one relates it, as one should, to its moment of appearance and to the acts which teach which form of grandeur it could be the source for. If some effect of the natural character of creative consciousnesses is felt at the origin of these forms, it is what remains and must remain indiscernible. The criterion of authenticity remains the same. It is that of a kind of consubstantiality between the idea and its act as well as between each and the concrete being of the person in the intimateness of his feelings as in his effective operations. As soon as the doctrine seems to dominate the witnesses, which are nothing but illustrations, an ideal form is constituted which tends to break off from history or ask from it only what are always somewhat imperfect expressions of an eternal essence. This ideal tends to make us forget that there is no other truth for us than the simultaneous promotion of thought and concrete being. Besides, nothing keeps us from conceiving the incompatibility of certain virtues and of certain inner dispositions of feeling as related to the kind of rivalry which these forms of grandeur arouse. It is related to the analysis which they effect in the human soul. Nor does anything prevent us from conceiving that other creations remain possible, as powerful for overcoming this hostility and for promoting new alliances and new groupings between qualities which today seem to be unaware of one another. In these other creations resignation would no longer contradict hope, nor renunciation the spirit of enterprise, nor purity the expansion of being and plenitude. The contingency of these creations would manifest better the contingency of the forms which today tend to compartmentalize moral and religious life. Just as moral invention at a certain level effects a conciliation between duties which opposed one another or were obstacles for one another in the hardening of their formulas, so likewise the creation of new forms of grandeur, by ordering all movements of the human soul to a new value and to a new doctrine, overcomes the apparent incompatibility of certain possibilities of existence. We often attempt to conciliate these possibilities by bringing into play a law of alternation as one passes from religious acts to life in the world or from this latter to an entirely esthetic contemplation of the possibilities of existence condemned to remain unreal but which give a kind of horizon to our own action.

Nevertheless, sometimes one feels that today, at the beginning of an age which could be an era of intense moral creation, one has a presentiment, in certain kinds of dedication which we accept as absolute actions, of real possibilities of existence for which the forms of grandeur to which we are accustomed are no longer adequate. One can define them only negatively by saying that in them sacrifice does not injure self-mastery, nor enthusiasm lucidity, nor the will for temporal goals detachment from the world. We discern badly the central value which commands this regrouping of values, and this undoubtedly is so because it is itself in correlation with profound changes in the goals and organization of social life. It prepares their advent as much as it is evoked by them. Nevertheless, what appears more clearly within these existences dedicated to actions which sanction their authority is a new relationship of nature to morality, including neither disdain nor indifference nor hostility with respect to tendencies and instincts. It includes no submission to their power but recognition of their strength and aid as a more decisive proof of the alliance sealed between nature and an aspiration in which the unconditionality of the primary affirmation is inscribed. There is no better sign of this alliance than the peace and transparency introduced into the most spontaneous feelings of the human soul.

When absolute actions imply willingness to lose one's life, they arouse our highest veneration. The feeling of moral sublimity which takes hold of us is concentrated on beings in which it appears that the spontaneity of instincts is radically reversed in favor of a consciousness which has equaled itself by acceptance of sacrifice. The supreme guarantee of a belief, the identity, finally verified, between the act interior to thought and a real action, the concentration of will in an act which consumes all the energy of a being, a victory over death won by death itself: it is all this that calls forth our veneration by reminding us of the truth of our own being, arousing in us both humility and the feeling of participation in a dignity which infinitely transcends us. We cannot refuse affirmation of these absolute actions nor close ourselves to their sublimity without at once feeling our self-attention weaken and relax. It is incumbent upon us then not only to save these actions from oblivion but to free them unreservedly from all relativity to conditions which would betray the act from which they issue. As soon as we begin to attribute to nature and to consciousness what belongs to each, we forbid ourselves the possibility of the humblest act. It is not by diminishing determinism that one raises oneself to these absolute actions; it is by resolutely posing them as transcendent to all explanation. The unconditionality of what is for us idea, that is, infinite exigency, authorizes us to do it and to judge our advance in existence by these actions. The same act by which we refuse for ourselves any pretension to be equal to what primary certitude requires of us envelops the legitimacy of our affirmation of absolute actions and guarantees the value of the feeling of sublimity which we first of all experience. These actions testify to the identity of an inner act and a concrete action which absorbs nature into itself, one might say, while depending on it.

It is not a question here of idolatry manifested in public by acclamations of a man and by blind submission of the will and the human spirit. It is rather a question of inner veneration, master of its choice, protected against all collective and emotional involvement. This veneration is inspired by the feeling that the being which we venerate is worthwhile beyond all value through that which is in fact beyond all value and that we go through it toward what is at the origin of our own being. It presents us with what reflection had us affirm.

This is why there is no higher power than that of veneration for the concrete progress of existence. Veneration implements and propagates the meaning of the decisive moments in which history is one with doctrine and act with idea. No will can will or be worthwhile except by appropriating the content of what consciousness knows first of all through veneration. Through veneration possibilities of existence are created, and even life in conformity with reason is inspired by it. The strength and the secret of the power of veneration are in the contact which it maintains with actions in which we cannot isolate, except reflectively and artificially, the initiative which has entered history and that which this initiative issues from and which transcends it. Moral and religious categories by which we judge, values by which we appreciate, the very rules themselves which we obey, in the most impersonal character they take on and in their permanence, must be related to highly contingent initiatives. They are contingent, of course, because of the act which they envelop, not because of the source which they incarnate.

For our own life, veneration intensifies the attention we give to those of our actions which symbolize as much as possible our fundamental certitude. It is nature as such which regains territory in all interruptions of this attention, in all the intervals left by actions which in some way witness for us. But it is not impossible, undoubtedly, that up to the very end of life itself the weakest reserve of energy which we owe to it could be consumed for goals over which life has no hold. This liaison between consciousness and the natural rhythm of life must still endure. Death can acquire immanent meaning only through this liaison. It is not that the *raison d'être* of life must be sought for in the relationship which it maintains with consciousness. This relationship is subordinated to it. Nor is death inscribed in our life so that we should consider it as a simple passage or as a test. Life and death must at first remain free of any such hypothesis. An initial depreciation of life can only radically falsify the judgment consciousness makes of death. Even more, such depreciation would rob death in advance of all its value. If consciousness, while it freely welcomes the thought of death, only ratified an earlier condemnation of life, the reasons for which this thought of death is accepted would add nothing to those which had us already condemn life. This latter emptied motives of their substance, in which consciousness found its courage or its faith. There is no longer any decision whose final meaning should not be sought in this initial judgment of life. The value of absolute actions abhors this idea, which would make us doubt whether they had been inspired by devotion to values incommensurable with life or if they had only found in these values a supplementary reason to justify a death already hoped for as such.

Principally, however, the veneration, inspired in us by beings in whom moral sublimity has shone forth, nourishes and maintains in us a feeling which detaches us from self-interests. A peace is produced which takes away the passional character from both enjoyment and pain. It erases in them what is local and partial and produces in them a transmutation of meaning. While stimulating our attachment to causes which wait on our devotedness, veneration brings to birth in the fringes of the emotions which accompany success or failure a feeling which detaches us from them. This experience would have no substance or truth without its liaison with life and effort. But it gives us access to an existence which owes its being neither to life nor to effort. It is the feeling that because of the unfolding of consciousness in duration there is discovered and created for itself, behind the man who is in sorrow and pain, a being which is touched neither by unfulfillment of his work nor by limitations of any order which impose the laws of life on his activity. It is a being which brings the experience of a certitude which transcends history to bear on the interruption of its history. Undoubtedly, this experience annexes to itself the immanent eternity of intelligence which understands but it is not identical with it. Only an act of reflection is necessary for the operation of thought to be duplicated in a consciousness of the eternal. But this reflection, renewable identically in every instant, is not susceptible of enrichment. In truth, it is a stranger to the effort of the inner being to be equal to itself. This reflection is without link with death, absence, or separation. Pretending to consider indifferently all that concerns only the self, it moves about on the level of an always actual correlation between time and the eternal which involves in no way the concrete decisions of consciousness and the real acceptance of loss. All that is necessary to raise oneself to the idea of the experience of the eternity of thought is a reflective grasping of the intellectual act. It is an element, but not the only element, of a deeper experience which gives us access to our true being, to a being which would remain hidden from us as long as we did not succeed in integrating death in our own history and in tearing it away from the natural course of our life. We then experience a regeneration which knows itself exposed to a rhythm of weakness and exaltation but which draws on this tension for a certitude surer of itself. This serenity is the substitute for eternity; it is all the eternity conceivable for a consciousness endeavoring to be equal to itself. This consciousness is able to do only by borrowing the forces of the individual and by the verifications which it effects and which are for it the symbols of an impossible adequation. This serenity shines on life itself. It creates the sweetness and depth of life. Serenity is the foretaste of what must rigorously remain unverifiable.